T0329021

GIRTON COLLEGE STUDIES

Edited by Lilian Knowles, Litt.D., Reader in Economic History in the University of London

No. 1

COMMERCIAL RELATIONS

OF

ENGLAND AND SCOTLAND
1603—1707

COMMERCIAL RELATIONS

OF

ENGLAND AND SCOTLAND
1603–1707

BY

THEODORA KEITH
B.A. TRIN. COLL. DUBLIN
OF GIRTON COLLEGE, CAMBRIDGE

WITH A PREFACE BY

W. CUNNINGHAM, D.D.
ARCHDEACON OF ELY

Cambridge:
at the University Press
1910

CAMBRIDGE
UNIVERSITY PRESS

University Printing House, Cambridge CB2 8BS, United Kingdom

Published in the United States of America by Cambridge University Press, New York

Cambridge University Press is part of the University of Cambridge.

It furthers the University's mission by disseminating knowledge in the pursuit of education, learning and research at the highest international levels of excellence.

www.cambridge.org
Information on this title: www.cambridge.org/9781107626621

© Cambridge University Press 1910

First published 1910
First paperback edition 2014

A catalogue record for this publication is available from the British Library

ISBN 978-1-107-62662-1 Paperback

PREFATORY NOTE

I WISH gratefully to acknowledge my indebtedness to Girton College for the award of the Cairnes Scholarship which enabled me to write this thesis, and also for the grant for its publication; to the London School of Economics for the opportunities for research work provided by it; to Archdeacon Cunningham for very kindly reading and criticising the manuscript; to Mr Hubert Hall, of the Public Record Office, and to the Rev. John Anderson, of the General Register House, for kind help; and especially to Dr Lilian Knowles, Reader in Economic History in the University of London, for constant help and encouragement.

THEODORA KEITH.

8 *July* 1910.

PREFACE

ENGLAND and Scotland are very different from one
another, both religiously and politically, and we
are apt to form an impression that the development of
each nation was separate and distinct, while occasional
incidents brought them into conflict. On closer consideration, however, this view of the relations of England
and Scotland appears inadequate; they are indissolubly
linked together as parts of the same island; there are
similar elements in the population of each, and they have
been affected by the same influences from time to time.
They have had so much in common throughout their
history that any movement, which took place in one, has
reacted, in some fashion, upon parties and affairs in the
other realm. The influence of the more advanced upon
the smaller country has been patent all along, for conscious
efforts have been made, again and again, to organise the
Scottish kingdom on an English model. On the other
hand, the effect of the political affinities of Scotland on
the schemes of English monarchs can never be left out of
sight; and the influence of popular movements in Scotland,

on the affairs of Church and State in England, becomes obvious in the Elizabethan and Stuart periods. By keeping this constant and intimate interconnection in mind we may sometimes get a clue to guide us through a maze of incidents that seem to be capricious and unintelligible.

From this point of view the commercial relationships, which Miss Keith has described so clearly and so fully, are particularly instructive. The study of the material interests of large sections of the population in both countries, brings into light motives which we may easily overlook unless attention is specially called to them. The bearing of merchants' grievances on questions of constitutional privilege was indirect and remote, and such topics rarely formed the theme of pulpit eloquence; but for all that, they were of extraordinary importance. The consideration of them helps us to understand why two countries, which were so closely associated and had so much in common, were kept apart; as well as to see the nature of the difficulties which had to be faced, when they were brought under one Crown. So far as religious and political affairs were concerned, close affinities existed between parties in Scotland and parties in England, and they were drawn into correspondence and sympathy; in the seventeenth century there was good reason, from time to time, for hoping that similar institutions, civil and ecclesiastical, might be established in each country. It almost seems as if the conduct and prospects of trade furnished the main reasons why Englishmen and Scots rallied into separate and hostile camps. Commercial interests united the people of each country in a common antagonism to their neighbour, and commercial jealousies kept these neighbours apart.

It is almost inevitable that two adjacent countries, with similar products and similar opportunities for industry, should be rivals in trade; but the commercial jealousy between England and Scotland became much more pronounced when they were brought into closer connection with each other by the Union of the Crowns. Trade relationships in these days were closely dependent on political affinities. When the two countries were ruled over by one monarch, the relations of friendship and hostility with foreign powers came to be the same for both; the Scots ceased to have opportunities for trade in places from which Englishmen were practically excluded, and the Scots merchants were forced to try and compete in markets where English traders had established their footing. There had been an ancient amity between France and Scotland; and Scots merchants had had privileges in French ports, such as Englishmen did not enjoy. The religious and political revolution in Scotland in the time of Queen Mary need not in itself have caused a rupture in this long established mercantile intercourse; but when Scotland was practically forced to follow the line of English policy, in regard to relationships with foreign powers, it was impossible for her to maintain her separate commercial privileges; Scots and English merchants were brought into direct competition with one another in the same markets.

There is nothing, with the exception of a foreign invasion, which brings home to the ordinary citizen the

results of government action so effectively as an interruption or decline in commerce. Miss Keith has shewn
in detail how deep was the influence of the disabilities
under which Scots trade laboured even in the reigns of
James I and Charles I, and still more under the diverse
policies of Cromwell and Charles II. The merchants in
the towns, and their dependents would be the first
sufferers, but industry would be affected as well; and
in the case of Scotland, which exported wool and raw
products, the effect would be felt far and wide. A sense
of grievance against England must have penetrated very
deeply; neither the policy of the first Stuart kings, nor
the free trade conditions of the Inter-regnum conciliated
the Scots, while the legislation of the Restoration Parliament was hostile to their interests. This aspect of the
case has been too much left out of sight, and Miss Keith
has rendered a real service by bringing it into prominence.
Much stress has been laid on the influence of religious
conviction—the opposition to Laud and the sufferings of
the Covenanters—in contributing to the failure of the
Dual Monarchy; but account should also be taken of the
fact that the conditions it brought about in Scotland were
unfavourable to business.

While this study of the commercial relations of
England and Scotland throws such interesting side lights
on political history, it is also of special interest with
regard to the economic life of both countries. Since the
time of Edward I the industrial and commercial progress
of the two nations had proceeded on distinct lines; when
the two were brought into contact, we can see more

clearly how far the institutions of the two peoples
differed, and learn to contrast the working and policy
of each with greater precision. Scotland was on the
whole a more backward country, and was certainly
much less flourishing than England; but so far as her
commercial institutions were concerned, it may be said
that Scotland was in some ways the more advanced of
the two. The Elizabethan and Stuart period in England
is marked by the superseding of municipal exclusiveness,
and the introduction of a system of national economy.
In Scotland municipal supervision of the products of
industry continued to be practised till the nineteenth
century; but so far as commerce is concerned, Scotland
had long enjoyed the means of regulating it on national
lines, in the Convention of the Royal Burghs. The combined trading in regulated companies, which was such
a characteristic feature of English commerce, had never
become an established Scots practice; Scotland moved
from medieval to modern trade organisation without
passing through this transitional form. The exclusive
status of the merchant was not carefully maintained, so
far as Scots merchants, in foreign parts, were concerned:
common sailors and others were accustomed to do a little
trading on their own account at the ports they visited;
and Scots pedlars found openings in the internal trade
of foreign countries. From the point of view of the
English Merchant Companies, the Scots were a nation
of interlopers; and it seems probable that they played
a considerable part in connection with the successive
attacks which went on throughout the seventeenth

century, both at home and abroad, on the exclusive privileges of the Regulated Companies. Scots commerce, like Scots banking in the eighteenth century, offered to self-reliant young men, opportunities which were not so generally available for those born south of the Tweed.

Miss Keith has been fortunate in choosing a subject which is of so much interest both in regard to political and to economic history; and she is to be congratulated on her success in dealing with a mass of material in such a fashion as to bring out the far-reaching importance of the details to which she has given so much care and thought.

W. CUNNINGHAM.

July 1910.

CONTENTS

INTRODUCTION

THE peace and prosperity of the Scotland of the early
middle ages were rudely broken in upon by the War of
Independence, at the beginning of the fourteenth century.
Not only were trade and industry interrupted and the
most fertile parts of the country laid waste, but the re-
adjustment of Scotland's international relations, resulting
from the war, prevented her recovery, and checked her
development. For more than two centuries she remained
at enmity with England, while her alliance was sought
and gained by England's other opponent, France. This
change in her circumstances had a disastrous effect upon
Scottish economic development. Her southern district
was in constant danger from English raids or Scottish
reprisals, and this, owing to the care of the great monastic
establishments, had been one of the most prosperous parts
of the kingdom. Her trade with England was interrupted,
and her population had to keep themselves in readiness
for military service. The frequent minorities of her kings,
and the feuds of the nobles with each other and with their
sovereign also combined to hinder Scottish economic progress in the fourteenth and fifteenth centuries. Friendship
with France did, however, bring some commercial advantages, for the Scots merchants obtained considerable

trading privileges there, especially in the province of Normandy, which they chiefly frequented.

Not until the middle of the sixteenth century did any substantial change occur in these relationships. In 1560 the Scottish Estates met in Convention adopted Protestantism as the national religion. Of this momentous decision Professor Hume Brown says : " Had Scotland remained a Roman Catholic country, the Union of the Crowns could hardly in the nature of the case have taken effect, and the Union of the Parliaments would have been excluded alike by the laws of God and man." This adoption by Scotland of the Reformed Religion was the first step towards a breach with France. A further step in the same direction was the Union of the crowns of England and Scotland in 1603, in the person of James VI. Scotland was now bound to England by the ties of common sovereignty and a common religion, while her ancient friendship and her commercial interests still attached her to France. Her principal trade also was with the Dutch, England's great commercial rivals of the seventeenth century.

It was not however in this direction only that the economic interests of the two countries did not harmonize. Scotland's economic development was far more backward than that of England. She was, says Professor Hume Brown, backward in " breaking away from the traditions of mediaevalism[1]." " In Scotland the hard and fast regulations which had bound the mediaeval merchant were as rigidly enforced as ever, whereas in England the door was virtually thrown open to all and sundry who might desire to put their capital to profitable uses[2]." Industry in Scot-

[1] *Scotland in the time of Queen Mary*, P. Hume Brown, p. 194.
[2] *Ibid.*, p. 195.

land was still controlled by the Craft Gilds, and organisation
and method were alike mediaeval. Manufactures were
little developed, and the chief exports were raw materials.
The countries, therefore, required different commercial
regulations. This was one reason why the Union of 1603
could not be complete; it was neither parliamentary nor
commercial, the crowns alone were united. The chief
reason for the backwardness of development in Scotland
was the lack of capital. Her soil was poor; also her
situation, remote from the ordinary course of European
trade, was a drawback to her. During the latter part of
the seventeenth century a change came about. The Scots
found themselves favourably placed for the new trade with
the West. Companies were founded to promote industry,
partly with the help of English capital. Scotland's
economic history in the seventeenth century is that of her
development into a modern state, which, though she could
not be a successful rival to England, could and did force
her greater neighbour to grant to her commercial equality.

During the seventeenth century the relationship established in 1603 became more and more unsatisfactory, and
this was greatly due to the conflicting economic interests
of the two countries. The English suffered from the
Union in four particular directions. These were, firstly,
the French trade ; where the English merchants were
jealous of the Scottish privileges in France during the
first years of the century, while during the latter part
they objected to the Scots maintaining their trade connection with a country with whom England was at enmity.
Secondly, the Dutch trade was a source of grievance, for
the English always feared that the Dutch merchants
through their connection with Scotland, might obtain

some share in English carrying trade, particularly in that to the Plantations. For, thirdly, after the Restoration the Scots gradually established an illegal trade with America, which was an offence against the English commercial system as embodied in the Navigation Acts. Fourthly, difficulties arose because of the different regulations as to import and export, which made the smuggling of certain commodities across the Borders a profitable occupation.

Scotland also suffered from the Union, especially in her foreign trade. Partly because of her connection with England she gradually lost her privileges in France. Her trade to France, and also to Holland, was interrupted and sometimes stopped by English wars with these countries, from which the Scots derived no benefit. She felt these checks to her trade especially towards the end of the century, when her industries developed, and when, as a crowning grievance, she was allowed no legal share in the English Plantation trade.

The century between the Unions of 1603 and 1707, treated chronologically, falls into three periods. James was anxious for an incorporating union, but neither nation was as yet ready to make the necessary concessions. During the first period, therefore, the reign of James I and part of that of Charles I, trade between the two countries was not free. James's subjects in England, Scotland, and Ireland, were, however, allowed to trade as natives, not as aliens, with any of the three countries. On the whole, however, there was little increase of intercourse between the countries. The most important feature of the period was that, although Scotland did succeed in retaining her privileges in France, the connection between these two countries gradually became less close.

Scotland suffered very much during the Civil Wars, and consequently the establishment of a complete Union under the Commonwealth in 1654 found her in an exhausted and poverty stricken state. Owing to this fact and also to the short duration of the Union it is difficult to estimate its possible results, had conditions been different. As matters stood the Union in this second period was unsatisfactory to both parties. England found the maintenance of an army, garrisons, and the civil government in Scotland a very heavy drain on her resources, while Scottish trade was hampered by the enforcement of English regulations as to import and export and navigation, and also by the wars of the Commonwealth with Holland.

As a result neither nation after the Restoration wished to continue this close relationship, and accordingly England and Scotland again became, but for their common king, separate countries. This third period is by far the most interesting. In it the English commercial system was further developed, and more strictly enforced, and France also developed a strong protective system. Scotland, by the action of the English Parliament, and by the loss of her privileges in France, was shut out from the advantages of both. At the same time the Scots became more anxious to develop industry and trade. They found themselves, however, greatly hampered by want of markets. Heavy duties hindered their trade with England, and by successive Navigation Acts they were excluded from any lawful share in the Plantation trade. They were partly shut out from the French trade by Colbert's protective measures, and their old privileges there were lost. For this they blamed their connection with England.

But on the other hand they still had some French trade, and they continued this connection during William's wars with France, in spite of the indignation and remonstrances of the English government and merchants. The English manufacturers joined in the complaints because the Scots supplied France and other continental countries with English wool. The export of wool from England was prohibited, but the Scots carried it over the border, and, the export of wool from Scotland being generally allowed, they took it abroad to be used in the cloth manufactories of England's commercial rivals. In spite of the Navigation Acts the Scots built up a considerable trade with the Plantations. To this the English most strongly objected, not only because Scotland supplied herself, and might in time supply other countries, with Plantation products, instead of getting them from England, but also because they feared that Dutch ships might trade with the Plantations under cover of the Scots connection.

Towards the end of the century it became more and more obvious to the thinking men of both countries that the relationship in its present state could not continue, and the episode of the Scots East India Company served to intensify this feeling. The Scots were determined to secure for themselves some market. The extensive privileges obtained by a Scots company from the Scots Parliament alarmed alike those interested in the East India and in the Plantation trades, while the results of the Darien expedition threatened to involve England in political difficulties with Spain. In both countries popular feeling ran very high, and it was now felt on all sides that some change must be made. Owing to the development of Scottish industry it was no longer necessary that the commercial regulations for the two countries should differ. In fact, Scotland had also built up a protective system very much on the lines of those of England and France, and partly in retaliation for her treatment by those countries. At this time the question became complicated by political considerations—England had settled the succession on the Hanover line, and feared that the Scots might refuse to co-operate with them and might recall the Stewarts, and that thus French influence would again become predominant in Scotland. In order, therefore, to consolidate and secure her commercial system, and to ensure the succession of the same sovereign in both kingdoms, England was willing to admit Scotland to commercial equality, while Scotland, anxious to secure markets for her manufactures, consented to merge her Parliament with that of England. Thus over a century of misunderstanding and dispute was brought to an end, and, very largely for commercial reasons on both sides, that Union was accomplished which has done so much to promote the prosperity and success of both kingdoms.

LIST OF ABBREVIATIONS

Royal Burghs = Records of the Convention of the Royal Burghs
    of Scotland.

S. P. Domestic = State Papers Domestic.

S. P. Col. = State Papers Colonial.

S. P. C. R. = Register of the Scottish Privy Council.

Acts, Scotland = Acts of the Parliament of Scotland.

H. M. C. R. = Historical Manuscripts Commission Report.

CHAPTER I

UNION OF 1603

a. CONDITION OF TRADE AT THE TIME OF THE UNION OF THE CROWNS

IN spite of the political and religious disturbances in Scotland in the sixteenth century, the trading community seem to have been able to carry on their business without much interruption and with some success. But their trade was curiously unaffected by those influences which were doing so much to transform the economic organisation of other European countries—the discovery of America and the consequent influx of silver. Capital was still extremely scarce in Scotland and manufactures were in a very backward condition, as also was agriculture. A paper amongst the manuscripts of the Earl of Mar and Kellie gives some idea of the commodities in which the Scots dealt and of the extent of their industrial development. It is entitled the "Table of Scottish Produce exported yearly[1]," and gives a list of all the commodities exported in the year 1614, together with their value. The "commodaties of

---

[1] *Historical Manuscripts Commission Report*, Mar and Kellie Papers, pp. 70—74.

the land" are the most valuable exports, amounting to
£375,085 Scots. These include different kinds of grain,
some flour and beef, £37,655; hides, £66,630; skins,
£172,082; wool, £51,870; feathers, butter, lead ore, coal,
£46,850. The value of the manufactures is £169,097, of
which salt, cloth and plaiding, and linen yarn are the
most important. The others mentioned are linen cloth,
coarse cloth, knitted hose, dressed leather, gloves, leather
points, sewed cushions, ticking for beds, shoes. The export
of fish brings £753,354, and of foreign commodities imported and then exported again, £39,047. The total value
for the year is £736,986 Scots. This does not include the
"greit quantitie of lynning claythe, lynning yairne, sheip,
nott etc. that is transpoirtted be land dalie," presumably
to England. The most important exports were therefore
unmanufactured commodities, skins, hides and fish, and
the manufactures exported were those of an economically
undeveloped country.

There were no companies of merchants organised for
trading to particular places, as the English Merchants
Adventurers, Eastland Company, etc. But the merchants
of the Royal Burghs practically formed an exclusive and
privileged company, for only they were allowed to engage
in foreign trade. The Convention of the Royal Burghs
looked after their interests, organising and supervising all
the foreign trade of the country; appointing conservators
to watch over Scottish interests in different places; settling
disputes between merchants; and even making regulations
concerning their clothing. In 1529, because many merchants trading with France and Flanders "takis with tham
thar evill and wirst clais to the dishonour of the realme,"
the conservator in Flanders was ordered to insist on their

providing for themselves " honest clais," and in case they should refuse he was entitled to seize and sell their goods, and with the proceeds to procure and pay for suitable garments[1]. Scottish merchants seem to have had a reputation for " parsimony in apparrell and dyet and...exceeding industriousness and diligence." They had not been at war with any continental nations for a long time, and their ships therefore did not require to be equipped for war as well as for trade. They were as a rule smaller than English ships, required less ballast, and in proportion to their size and the expense of sailing them, could take in a larger cargo and charge a smaller freight rate. Another reason for the cheapness of their freight was the way in which the crew lived. " The Scotts marriners go not to sea as our men goe everyone for wages in certainty and feeding on the Victueller or Owner on the best Beefe Porke Beere Biskett of the finest Wheat and to care not what they spoile of the owners..., nor how long time they protract in making their Voyage and Return. But every-one...finds himself the whole Voyage eates no Bread but Oaten Cakes made of Bean baked on the hearth and salt ffish fryed on the Coales from hand to mouth by himself, nor weares no Cloaths eyther Lynnen or Woollen (which are very mean) but those of their own countrey makeing and at cheapest Rate....And besides...everyone in their ships...is a kind of Merchant himself and will be sure to bring some Lynnen Scotch Cloth...or Such like from home upon his own Account and make a like Returne of some Commodities which the fforeyn Markett yeildeth. Whereas in our English Shipps they are not much given

[1] *Records of the Convention of the Royal Burghs of Scotland*, I., p. 509.

to this thriveing course as they are prohibited by the
Merchants that fraight them to do it, for the marring
of the Merchants own Markett....The Scotts Owners of
Shipps and Mariners will be able and readie to undergoe
a freight to any forreyn parte for under our Owners rate,
and yet by these meanes gain whereas ours loose by it[1]."
A good deal of the Scots foreign trade seems to have
been carried on by pedlars, who, when their ship reached
port, travelled up and down the country with their packs,
selling to the country folk, like the Breton onion sellers
of to-day. The crew of the ship may also have taken
part in this peddling trade.

The Scots in their small ships did not penetrate very
far afield. Their commercial connections were chiefly with
France, Spain, the Low Countries, and the Baltic. There
was also some trade with England. The French and Dutch
trades engaged more merchants and ships than any other.
There had long been a close connection between Scotland
and France, commercial as well as political. According to
one authority, the first commercial treaty had been made
by Achaeus and Charlemagne in 787. Coming to more
modern times however, in 1510 Francis I exempted the
Scots nation from the payment of customs in Normandy.
This was confirmed by Henry II in 1554, and at the same
time the Scots were exempted from the payment of some
new duties then imposed[2]. Four years later, when Mary
was married to the Dauphin, all Scotsmen were made
naturalised subjects in France and all Frenchmen in

---

[1] *The Union of England and Scotland*, British Museum, Harleian
MSS. 1314.

[2] *Royal Burghs*, ii., p. 576. *Les Écossais en France*, Francisque
Michel, i., p. 357.

Scotland[1]. Scots merchants were therefore free from all
impositions laid upon strangers. These privileges were
all confirmed by Henry IV in 1599[2]. The Scots traded
chiefly to Normandy, Bordeaux and La Rochelle, taking
thither wool, skins, hides, plaiding, kerseys, salmon, and
bringing back wines and salt[3]. A number of Scottish
ships were also engaged in the carrying trade for France.
In 1615 it was said that "the greittest number of the
best schippis of Scotland ar continuallie imployed in the
service of Frenchmen, not only within the dominions of
France, bot also within the boundis of Spayne, Italie and
Barbarie[4]."

Trade with the Low Countries was also important.
The Convention of the Royal Burghs received privileges
for their merchants there by a contract with some city,
which was then called the Scots Staple Port, to which
certain specified commodities, including all the most important Scottish exports to the Netherlands, had first to
be brought. Certain privileges were granted to the Scots
merchants in Flanders in the fourteenth century, but the
first definite treaty with Scotland was made by Bruges
in 1407. This city was the headquarters of the Scots
merchants during the greater part of the fifteenth century,
though they also traded with Middelburg, and the Staple
was for a time established there. In 1506 some arrangement was made with Campvere, and after competition on
the part of Middelburg, Antwerp and Campvere for the
monopoly of Scots trade, the Staple was fixed at Campvere

[1] *Royal Burghs*, IV., p. 500. *Les Écossais en France*, I., p. 303.
[2] *Ibid.*, II., p. 577.
[3] *Early Travellers in Scotland*, ed. P. Hume Brown, p. 87.
[4] *Letters and State Papers of James VI*, p. 213.

in 1541. There it remained with but two short intervals until the Staple contract was cancelled in 1799[1]. Scottish shipping seems to have been considerable in the sixteenth century, if the following incident may be believed. During Charles V's wars with Francis I, the Scots, although they were considered neutral, seized some English ships at Campvere. The Emperor then ordered his subjects in the Netherlands to make reprisal upon them, but "the Scots likeweys equipped, and were so much superior at Sea (which will now hardly gain credit) that they not only confined the Dutch and Flemish Privateers in their harbour, but interrupted the Trade of those of the Provinces, Flanders, Zealand and Holland, and of the great city Antwerp itself[2]." The principal commodities which the Scots took to the Netherlands were cloth, skins, wool, fish and salt. They received a good deal of soap, corn and hardware, and a number of miscellaneous articles. There was also some trade between the ports on the east coast, Aberdeen, Dundee, the Fife ports and Leith, and the northern countries, Norway, Sweden, Denmark, and the Baltic ports. Of this trade we have valuable information in the *Compt Buik of David Wedderburne*[3], a Dundee merchant. The Baltic ports which the Dundee ships chiefly frequented were Dantzig and Königsberg, and also Stralsund and Lübeck. The imports into Scotland were principally timber, iron, flax, hemp, pitch and tar.

During the sixteenth century there was a good deal of intercourse between Scotland and Spain. In 1581

---

[1] For the history of the Staple and Scottish trade with Holland, see *Scottish Staple at Veere*, J. Davidson and A. Gray.

[2] *Historical Account of the Staple Contract between the Burrows of Scotland and Campvere*, 1749.

[3] *Compt Buik of David Wedderburne* (Scottish History Society).

" certan writis evidentis and privilegis granted be the King of Spain under his greit seill, for the weilfair of the Scotis natioun " were obtained[1]. The trade chiefly developed during the wars of England with Spain, when the English merchants traded with Spain under cover of the Scots trade. Several instances of this are given in the *Calendar of State Papers (Spanish)*. " Two Scotch Ships either have left or will shortly leave London....One of them is of 150 tons burden called the New Ship of St Andrews...loaded with wrought iron and tin and lead in pigs and a quantity of English serge. The goods bear the leaden seal of Edinburgh, but are made in England and the seal is placed on them to deceive....The other ship is from Little Leith...carries similar merchandize. The value of the cargoes is estimated at £14000." The Editor, in a note to this reference, says, " The above is given as a typical instance of the continual trade in English merchandize with Spain under cover of Scottish merchants during the period when all commercial communication between England and Spain was prohibited[2]." In 1603 the Venetian Secretary in London writing to the Doge, in reference to the question of peace with Spain, says that James I has often been helped with money by Spain, " especially before Spanish and Flemish commerce came to Scotland. It was then that the revenue which ordinarily did not exceed 100000 crowns, was greatly increased, as the King was able to tax the seaports[3],

---

[1] *Royal Burghs*, i., p. 126.

[2] *Calendar S. P., Spanish*, 1587–1603, No. 191.

[3] No tax was laid on imports into Scotland until 1597, when all merchandize was required to pay 12d. of every pound's worth. An *ABC* of the value of all wares was then drawn up, but was superseded in 1612 by a new book of rates.

which were growing rich, by imposing customs upon
wine and other commodities[1]." In another letter the
Secretary declares that the revenue in Scotland has increased to 400,000 crowns, "thanks to having an open
trade to France, Spain and all the northern countries."

The political connection with England before the Union
was slight, and the commercial relations of the two countries
were also of little importance. There was some trade in
linen cloth and yarn, salt and sheep from Scotland; and
from England were brought wheat, beer, bark, woollen
cloth, etc. The Scots frequented chiefly the ports of
London and Newcastle, but Plymouth and other harbours
in Devonshire and the West were also visited. There
was also some trade by land, but the disturbed state of
the Borders on either side made peaceful traffic difficult.
There was no Scots conservator in England, and though
the King suggested in 1599 that one should be appointed,
because of the complaints of merchants trading thither,
the Convention of Burghs declined to do so. They declared that a conservator was not "necessar to thair estait
bot rather hurtful and chargeabill to the samyn[2]." Some
figures given in "An Estimate of the Customes and
Subsidies of Tonnage and Poundage as well Inwardes as
Outewards payd by Scottishe Merchantes for VII yeares,"
from 1597 to 1603, shew that the trade was but small.
In London the duties inwards paid for the seven years
amounted to £743. 19s. 4d., and outwards to £595. 0s. 7d.
The duties paid at the outports were £1366. 18s. 6d. and
£1679. 12s. 6d. respectively[3]. In Scotland the customs

---

[1] *Calendar S. P., Venetian*, p. 69.

[2] *Royal Burghs*, II., p. 48.

[3] *S. P. Domestic, James I*, v., 47.

paid for a year, 1605–6, on the English trade were £1083, paid by Scots and English merchants[1].

As yet the Scots had not penetrated across the Atlantic. Fynes Moryson says that though the "Scots are very daring...they have not hitherto made any long voyages rather for want of riches, than for slothfulnesse or want of courage[2]." They had not yet been inspired by the general impulse of the sixteenth century to compete for the "golden ball of trade."

b. Negotiations for Commercial Union

James VI, on his succession to the throne of England, was extremely anxious that his two kingdoms should be fused into one homogeneous whole; that Scotland and England should lose their separate names and nationalities, and become the kingdom of Great Britain. For the first few years of his reign he made great endeavours to accomplish this end, but English hostility and Scottish indifference were too much for him, and with the growth of other interests in England the project was allowed to drop. One of James's first acts when he came to England was an "Act authorising certain Commissioners of the Realm of England to treat with Commissioners of Scotland for the weale of both Kingdoms[3]." Commissioners were appointed in Scotland also, and the two deputations met, discussed conditions and drew up a Treaty of Union, to be proposed to their respective Parliaments. Some of the articles were afterwards incorporated in the two acts—

[1] *Register of the Scottish Privy Council*, VII., p. 392.
[2] *Early Travellers in Scotland*, p. 87.
[3] 1 Jac. I, c. 2.

"An Act for the utter Abolition of all memory of Hostilitie
and the Dependances thereof between England and Scotland[1]," and "An Act anent the Union of England and
Scotland[2]." The latter declared "That all the particular
hostile Laws...maid be Scotland aganis England as Enemies
sall be abrogat and in all tyme cuming all utterlie extin-
guished." The other clauses of the treaty were not carried
into effect. A number of the articles dealt with the subject
of commerce, though an entire commercial union was not
suggested. It was proposed that there should be free
trade in the native commodities of either country, with
the exception of wool, sheep, sheepfells, cattle, leather,
hides and linen yarn. This "mutual liberty of exportation and trade" was to serve "for the inward use only
of either realm." Commodities of which the export or
import was prohibited for either country were to be
prohibited for both. Otherwise import and export were
to be free for subjects of either kingdom. Import from
France was excepted until inquiry should be made into
the extent of Scottish privileges there. Imported foreign
goods that had paid custom once were not required to
pay it again on passing from one country to another.
The fisheries within fourteen miles of the coast were to
be retained by each nation respectively. Merchants of
either country were to be allowed to join the companies
of the other, which meant that Scots merchants might
join English companies, as the Scots had no associations
of merchants[3]. Certain sources of future difficulties are

[1] 4 Jac. I, c. 1.

[2] *Acts of Parliament of Scotland*, IV., p. 466.

[3] For the clauses of the treaty see Spottiswoode, *History of the
Church of Scotland*, II., p. 148.

obvious in the conditions of this treaty. The customs rate differed in each country, being as a rule lower in Scotland. Therefore some foreign commodities paying duty in Scotland might be sold at a profit in England, where the duties on the same commodities were higher, although the cost of transport might equalise matters. The regulation of import and export in different interests by different authorities would always be a difficulty. English manufactures, for instance, were more developed than those in Scotland, and therefore the export of raw materials was restrained in England, whereas Scotland's chief trade was in unmanufactured goods.

The union project aroused much opposition amongst English merchants. They objected to the idea of any union at all, and in detail to almost every clause of the treaty. They declared that the Scots were so poor that their incorporation with the English trading community could be no benefit to England, for the "kingdom of Scotland noway affordeth commodities in any reciprocall course with England for trade and merchandising." The merchants said that they "do already of themselves vent all the Commodities of this land, and yet are they hardly able to live one by another. Quando minus therefore shall they be able if they admit such an unnumbered sort of people of another nation to intermingle themselves among them in an equall communion of commerce[1]." Also the Scots "trade after a meaner sort and condition in foreign parts than we, as by retailing parcels and remnants of cloth and other commodities up and down the countries as we cannot do because of the honour of our country." It was feared that poor Scots would flock to England "in

[1] British Museum, Harleian MSS. 1314.

such multitudes as that death and dearth is very probable
to ensue and wheresoever any artificer or tradesman of
that nation shall dwell or abide it is very likely that in a
short time he will gather unto himself the wealth of his
neighbours, and undermine them in profit as the horse
will undereat the ox such is their parsimonious life in
respect of ours and their poverty will be evermore a spur
unto them to make them industrious to thrive but to be
satisfied there is no hope for[1]." As an illustration of the
"parsimony and diligence of ye Scotch above ye English
nations," the following tale is told. At Dartmouth, "two
ships (the one English and the other Scotch) being both
ready to Wey Anker and bound for wyne at Burdeaux
the wind happening fair for them on M[as] Day the Scotch
accordingly weyed Anker, and hald over to his consort the
Englishman and asked him why he did not Wey Anker
accordingly So when the Englishman Answered I have
all my men on board and am ready but I have bid my
neighbours to a Mich[mas] Goose and I will goe but on shore
and eat it and come presently. In which little Interim
the Scotch Ship was no sooner freed of the Harbour but the
wind cast about, So as when the Englishman came aboard
after dinner he could not wind out of ye Harbour though
that wind Served the Scotchman at sea well enough.
About 6 weekes after the Scotch ship revened with her
full loading of Wine into the same Harbour upon the
foresaid Englishman haling for newes the Scotch answered
that they had brought Wine for their goose[2]." One would
conclude from this incident that the Scots were not given
to wasting their opportunities. Presumably, from the many

[1] *S. P. Domestic, James I*, x., 17.
[2] British Museum, Harleian MSS. 1314.

complaints as to their "mean way of trade," their expenses
were less and their profits greater in the few branches of
trade in which they came into contact with English
interests.

Passing from general to particular objections, English
merchants seemed to fear that the Scots would get cloth
from the northern counties more cheaply than their own
merchants in the south, would transport it abroad and
thus ruin their trade[1]. Also that the Scots would sell
English commodities which were not allowed to be exported, to French and Flemings in Scotland. Then, too,
the taxes and customs differed in the two countries, and
were as a rule higher in England than in Scotland. The
English merchants failed to see why the Scots, with fewer
burdens on their trade, should share English advantages[2].
The greatest obstacle, however, was the question of the
Scottish privileges in France. As has been said, the Scots
obtained the privileges of naturalisation in France in 1558,
and therefore traded on the same terms as natives of the
country. It was possible for English subjects to become
naturalised in France, but only on payment of a certain
fee, generally 100 crowns, and they were then regarded as
foreigners in England[3]. All Scotsmen, on the other hand,
were naturalised Frenchmen, and at the same time kept
their position as Scots subjects. The benefits accruing to
the Scots were considerable. They could hold offices and
acquire land in France, which the ordinary Englishman
could not do. They paid fewer impositions and customs,
only four pence in the pound; while the English merchant

---

[1] *S. P. Domestic, James I*, xxiv., 3, 10.

[2] *Journals of House of Commons*, i., p. 332.

[3] *S. P. Domestic, James I*, xxiv., 11.

paid the four pence, and two other impositions as well.
Also English merchants were only allowed to sell their
cloth at the Freehall at the ports to which they resorted.
Other goods had to be displayed for sale on the wharf
for a certain time, paying a rent meantime for using it.
Scots merchants could sell their goods in their ships or
anywhere else they pleased[1]. They could also buy goods
freely, and were permitted to sell them again in the
country. But the privileges for export were only observed for goods to be conveyed into Scotland; if they
were to be transported elsewhere, the Scots merchants had
to pay the same duties as other foreigners. Nevertheless,
the English feared that the Scots would undersell them in
the French trade.

Almost all objections made against a union were
answered, and the difficulties shewn not to be insuperable.
A proposal was even made to equalise the customs[2]. This
would have removed the principal obstacles in the way of
a commercial union at the time, but unless the union was
parliamentary as well, there could be no satisfactory
guarantee that either customs or regulations as to
imports and exports would remain the same in the
future. To inquire into the differences in the French
trade it was agreed that two representatives from either
side should be sent to Normandy to inform themselves
of the state of affairs there, and also in other parts of
France[3]. In the Bordeaux trade neither appeared to
have much advantage over the other. The work of the
commissioners was, however, vain as far as the discussions

---

[1] *S. P. Domestic, James I*, xxiv., 10.

[2] *Commons Journals*, i., p. 333.

[3] *Ibid.*, i., p. 322. *Register of the Scottish Privy Council*, vii., p. 473.

on commerce were concerned. The English Parliament only abolished all hostile laws against Scotland. In the Scottish Parliament the whole treaty was passed, but with the proviso that "the same should be in like manner ratified by the parliament of England, otherwise the conclusion taken should not have the strength of a law[1]." As England did not ratify the treaty, it never became valid in Scotland. One most important result of the Union was achieved, not by Parliament, but by the decision of the judges—the naturalisation in England of all Scotsmen born after James's accession to the English throne[2].

In fact neither nation was at this time at all anxious for a complete union. The merchants of London declared that "it cannot otherwise prove to be but an impoverishment to both nations and will in the sequell of time... turn also to the hurt and detriment of the state of both the kingdomes[3]." The Scots spoke of "that Union so greitlie hated by them," the English, "and so little affected by us"; and hoped that his Majesty "would be pleased to desist fro any further moving of this Union[4]." The mutual hostility of over three hundred years was not to be overcome merely by the accession of a Scottish king to the English throne. Bacon's vision of "England, with Scotland united, with Ireland reduced, with the Low Countries contracted, with Shipping maintained...the greatest Empire that hath been heard of in many Ages[5]" was not to be realised in the seventeenth century.

---

[1] Spottiswoode, II., p. 192.
[2] *History of Scotland*, J. Hill Burton, v., pp. 411—415.
[3] *S. P. Domestic, James I*, XXIV., 3.
[4] *Ibid.*, XXVI., 68.
[5] *Commons Journals*, I., p. 337.

Although the scheme for commercial union failed, there was for a few years, while the negotiations were being carried on, free trade between the two countries. The merchants of both countries seemed at once to conclude that James's accession in England of necessity brought with it freedom of trade. A Proclamation in November, 1603, declared that both Scots and English had transported goods by "fels and other by-passages," by which his majesty was defrauded of his customs. Therefore all goods were ordered to be sent by Berwick or Carlisle, or shipped at some known port[1]. The defrauding of the customs continued, and in 1605 and 1606 arrangements were made for books to be kept by the farmers of the customs in both countries, in which all goods passing from one country to the other were to be entered. These were to be compared every six months in order for the "escheiving of all fraud that may be useit heireftir[2]." Next year, however, James, "being myndit...to unite thir twa famous kingdomes under his Majesty's royall crowne and sceptour and to remove all markis of separatioun betwixt the same...in the mean-tyme of the treaty of this Unioun and for the better introduction of the Same," commanded that no customs should be taken for commodities transported between the kingdoms. Caution was to be taken for the payment of the customs in case "the same treaty tak not effect." The commodities which were freed from duties were to be only enough for the use of each country, not for

[1] S. P. Domestic, James I, Proclamation Collection, p. 55.

[2] S. P. Domestic, James I, xxvi., 50. Acts of the Parliament of Scotland, iv., p. 285.

exportation[1]. This policy was not found to be successful, and in 1611 the duties were reimposed again. It was found that not only did the King lose revenue, but goods which were not allowed to be exported from one country were secretly conveyed into the other and thence exported. Goods transported by land were therefore ordered to be taken through Berwick or Carlisle on the English side, and by Aytoun, Jedburgh, Kelso, Dumfries or Annan on the Scottish border[2].

Four years later another proclamation dealing with trade was issued. James declared that "ever sithence Our comming to the possession of the Imperial Crowne of the Kingdomes of England and Ireland, Our ful resolution and constant purpose and meaning was, and always hath beene by all good meanes to set forward and advance Trade, Trafique and Merchandize, aswell Within Our Kingdome of Scotland, as in Our Kingdomes of England and Ireland, and to augment and increase the Ships, Shippings and Navigation of the same Kingdomes of England, Scotland and Ireland for the Wealth; Strength and prosperitie of the same Kingdomes, And for that purpose and to give the better encouragement unto Our naturall Subjects of the said Kingdome of Scotland to set forward and increase their Trade." Therefore orders had been given that no other duties were to be paid by Scots ships or goods than were paid by English or Irish ships or goods, in England and Ireland, and the "Ilands under the Dominions of the same." Also Scottish ships were no longer to be considered "Strangers Bottomes but

---

[1] *Scottish Privy Council*, VII., pp. 347, 377.

[2] *S. P. Domestic, James I, Proclamation Collection*, p. 240. *Scottish Privy Council Register*, IX., pp. 263, 267.

free Bottomes." English and Irish ships and goods were
to have the same privileges in Scotland[1]. This was
confirmed by Charles I in 1631 in "a Proclamation for
enabling all His Majesties Subjects to Trade within His
Severall Dominions without being further charged with
Customes, or other dueties, than they of that Kingdome
wherein they trade, ought to pay[2]." Certain staple commodities were not allowed to be exported to Scotland.
In 1622 the exportation from England of "Woolles,
Woolle-fels, Yarne, Fullers earth, and Wood-ashes into
any forraine parts, or into Our Kingdome of Scotland"
was forbidden[3]. Apparently great quantities of hides
and leather were conveyed into Scotland, and in 1626
their transportation was also forbidden[4]. In 1632 the
transportation of these commodities, and also of corn, out
of England was prohibited[5]. During the reigns of the
first two Stewarts, therefore, the Scots and their ships
were treated as natives and not as aliens.

Under Commonwealth rule there was an approach to
a system of *laissez faire* and absence of regulation. In
this period Scotland was commercially united with
England, and there were no restrictions at all upon
trade between the two countries. With the Restoration
Parliament began to take a much larger share in the
regulation of economic affairs in both countries. The
English Parliament adopted a strong protective system.
As far as they could see free trade with Scotland neither

---

[1] *S. P. Domestic, James I, Proclamation Collection*, p. 39.

[2] British Museum. Proclamations, 506 *h.* 11 (3). *Scottish Privy
Council* (2nd Series), IV., p. 458.

[3] British Museum. Proclamations, 506 *h.* 12 (99).

[4] *Ibid.*, 506 *h.* 11 (85).   [5] *Ibid.*, 506 *h.* 12 (13).

had been nor could be of advantage to English commercial interests; they had no desire to promote Scottish prosperity, and, though Charles was anxious for a commercial union between the two countries, Scotland was treated as a foreign country by the legislation of the English Parliament. The Scottish Parliament also adopted a protective policy, and, in return for English restrictions, laid heavy burdens on English trade with Scotland. The first period of the seventeenth century, therefore, was more favourable to the interests of Scottish trade with England than the period of parliamentary regulation after the Restoration.

CHAPTER II

a. INDUSTRY IN SCOTLAND

JAMES, although his residence and court were removed to London, did not at all neglect the internal interests of his kingdom of Scotland. In fact after his accession in England, his authority in Scotland was more absolute than it had been before. The Privy Council was his instrument, and through it he carried out his schemes for the establishment of order, economic development, and ecclesiastical settlement in Scotland. The existence of a single authority for both kingdoms made an organised effort to suppress disorder on the Borders possible. There was no longer any danger of English or Scottish raids, and a Commission of five Englishmen and five Scotsmen was appointed to suppress feuds and establish order amongst the unruly Border clans. They carried out their instructions mercilessly, unscrupulously and thoroughly, with the result that it was said, with some truth, that the "Middle Shires" were "as lawful, as peaceable and as quiet as any part in any civil kingdom in Christianity." James also endeavoured to establish his authority and some degree of order in the Highlands and Islands. Peace on the border and some security from Highland raids naturally tended to encourage the Lowlanders in the pursuit of the arts of peace, and in this they received all encouragement from the government. As a result there was considerable economic activity in Scotland during the early part of the seventeenth century until the beginning of the religious struggles and the Civil Wars.

The encouragement and improvement of already established manufactures, the introduction of new methods, the regulation of import and export, and the interests of foreign trade all received the attention of the King and his Council. The development of the manufacture of cloth was a favourite project which had for some time occupied the attention of the authorities. Various efforts were made to improve it during the sixteenth century, and in 1597 the " hamebringing of Englis claith" was forbidden[1]. The production of native cloth was not however sufficient, and the prohibition was rescinded two years later[2]. In 1600, efforts were made to introduce foreign help to improve the manufacture. It was said that "the unskilfulness of our awin people heirtofoir, togidder with the unwillingnes to suffer ony strangeris to cum amangis thame, has bene ane of the caussis that hes hinderit" the growth of the manufacture of wool; "they being unhable, without the help of strangeris quha ar better acquent with that tred to attine to ony perfectioun in that work[3]." Liberty was therefore given for a hundred families of foreign cloth-workers to settle. They were to be naturalised, and made free burgesses of any burgh in which they should settle.

[1] *Acts, Scotland*, iv., p. 119.   [2] *S. P. C. R.*, vi., p. 521.
[3] *Ibid.*, p. 123.

Several families did immigrate, although they were not welcomed by the Scottish artisans.

In 1620 a patent was given to the town of Edinburgh for making cloths, and a long list is given of the different varieties which were made. Amongst them were "cairseyis," "freissis and kiltis," "quhyte cottounes," "bumbaseyis," "growgraynes," "cottoun Fustianis," "seargeis" etc., also some materials known by the strange names of "Stand-afar," "Over keik," and "Fair a far aff[1]." Three years later, in accordance with James's wishes as expressed in a letter to the Privy Council, a standing committee for manufactures was appointed, with a large scope for action. It was to consider chiefly the wool manufacture, what was needed for its encouragement, how new works should be set up, what variety of manufacture was best for home use, and what for exportation, whether foreigners should be brought in, and whether societies should be formed. On all these points the Committee was to confer, and then to "sett down ordinanceis thairanent[2]." The members however did not meet very often, and do not seem to have done very much in setting up new works or introducing new processes. The existing works were carried on very successfully. "Plaiding" was one of the most important of Scottish manufactured exports. In 1634 and 1635 there was much discussion as to the way in which it should be done up for sale. The manufacturers seem to have sold it in "hard rolls," not "open folds," so that the purchasers could not see what they were buying. This tended to give a bad name to Scots cloth abroad, and so the Council decided that it must be laid out for sale in folds for the

---

[1] *S. P. C. R.*, xii., pp. 337—339.   [2] *Ibid.*, p. 301.

buyers to examine. The other varieties of cloth which were made were more for home use than for export, and were not manufactured in any very large quantities. Some of these were new manufactures, brought in by the efforts of James and Charles; but their care resulted more in the increase of the quantity produced by the old methods than in the introduction of new cloth industries.

The question of the wool supply was an important problem during this period, and indeed throughout the seventeenth century. It was felt that, in order to encourage the cloth manufacture, the supply should be plentiful and the price low. But when the export was prohibited, complaints were at once made by the wool-growers, and also by the merchants and shippers, who declared that their trade abroad would be ruined. And as a matter of fact, the manufacturers were not, as a rule, able to use all the wool in the kingdom. Also wool was one of the principal exports, especially to Holland. It was therefore difficult for the Council or Parliament to decide on a definite policy, and in consequence the regulations varied from time to time. On the whole, perhaps the export was more often prohibited than allowed, but customs officials were neither strict nor numerous, and the laws prohibiting the export were more often than not entirely ignored.

The export of wool was forbidden in 1602, but the prohibition was evidently disregarded, for in 1612 and 1614 it was said that "woll hes bene transportit in verie grite quantities," and the prohibition was re-enacted[1]. In 1616 the matter was brought up before the Convention of Royal Burghs, who considered that "the haill countrey

[1] *S. P. C. R.*, VI., p. 521; IX., p. 409; X., p. 273.

woll mycht be wrogt at hame." At the same time, they
"planelie and flatlie refusit...to undertak any burdyne
in that mater." Nevertheless the export was prohibited
again. Although the efforts to encourage the cloth manufacture had been fairly successful, yet "since his sacred
Majestie's happy arryvall to the commandment of both
kingdomes by his Hienis solide government the store is
sua increased" that licences had of late been granted
for export. So in 1623 the whole question was most
exhaustively discussed, information being got from landowners and Justices of the Peace as to the price of wool
in different shires. The result was that export was again
prohibited, but, as before, licences were granted for transporting wool, and the prohibition gradually fell into
abeyance. Theoretical prohibition and practical freedom
therefore sum up the history of the export trade in wool
during the early part of the century.

The English Privy Council were exercised over the
same question, which later in the century became of very
great importance. In 1622 the export of wool from
England was forbidden, because the "Cloth & Stuffes
of this Our Kingdom, haue not that Vent in foraine parts
which formerly they haue had." In 1632 the export was
again forbidden. The discussions of this question illustrate
the different stages of economic development of the two
countries. The English export of cloth was of far greater
importance than the export of wool, and the export of
wool was forbidden in order that the cloth trade should
be maintained. In Scotland, on the other hand, the export of the raw material was a very important branch of
her trade, and, although a considerable amount of coarse
cloth was exported, the main object of the Scottish Council

was that sufficient cloth should be made to supply the home demand.

The freedom or restraint of the export of other products besides wool also came under consideration. The question of the export of several native commodities—coals, wool, cattle, etc.—and of the import of foreign victual came up before the Council in 1626, and the whole matter was discussed at great length. The burghs and people generally wanted restraint of export and free import; the landowners and coalowners desired free export and restricted import[1]. Finally, the export of victual was allowed when the prices were under certain fixed sums. The question of the free export of coal was one which had already received much attention. Complaints had often been made of its export on the grounds that the supply would become exhausted, and also that it raised prices for the home consumer. The Council now declared that the prices to Scottish dealers were to be 5s. per ton less than the price to foreigners, if they were going to sell it again by retail, and 2s. less if they were going to export it[2]. The rates on coal were doubled in 1634 to raise revenue, and also as a protection against exhaustion of the supply by too much exportation[3]. A few years later (1641) it was found that the "trade hath not only beene deserted by strangers in regarde of the said extraordinarie imposition; to the undoing of manie of our poore subjects who had thair subsistence thairby, bot also to the utter ruine of the maisters of the saide coale works." The extra duty was therefore taken off[4].

The reform of the tanning industry was another question

[1] *S. P. C. R.* (2nd Series), I., p. lxxxiv.
[2] *Ibid.*, pp. 275—280.   [3] *Ibid.*, IV., pp. 217, 258.
[4] *Ibid.*, VII., p. 160.

which occupied the attention of the Council. There were
many complaints about the quality of Scots leather due
to " the ignorance and unskilfulness of the tannaris." It
was suggested that twelve persons skilled in the " trew
and upright form of tanning" should be brought from
England for a year to introduce better methods[1]. Lord
Erskine was appointed undertaker in 1619, and had to
pay the expenses of bringing in the strangers, getting a
patent of monopoly of tanning for thirty-one years, and
receiving 4s. per hide sealed by him as good for twenty-
one years[2]. The Scottish tanners were not at all anxious
to receive instruction. The cordiners, who were for the
most part tanners, combined, "maligning and repineing
aganis this intendit reformatioun...and resolvit so far as
in thame lyis to croce and hinder the same, and to foister
and interteine thair former ignorance of the speciall pointis
of that trade." In order to " mak this intendit reformatioun seam distaistful to the people...they haif verie
extraordinarlie raised and highted the pryceis of thair
bootis and shoone[3]." The cordiners were at first successful in their resistance, for the Council declared in
1622 that " the whole panes tane thairin ar lyke to
prove void and ineffectuall[4]." A few years later, however, the development in the leather trade through the
improvement of tanning was noted, and there was an
agitation for free exportation of hides[5]. This was not
yet allowed, but licences were occasionally granted to
certain merchants or burghs to export some of their
stock of hides.

[1] S. P. C. R., xii., pp. 170—171.   [2] Ibid., xii., ix., x.
[3] Ibid., xii., p. 424.   [4] Ibid., p. 642.
[5] Ibid. (2nd Series), i., p. lxxxvii.

Several new industries and new processes were introduced during this period. In 1611 a monopoly for twenty-one years was granted to Nathaniel Udward for making linen cloth. He intended to bring in a number of strangers from Holland to introduce "the best making and usuall form and manner as is maid in Holland." Thus the yarn which was now exported and wrought abroad would be made up at home[1]. This Nathaniel Udward was a person of great activity, quite one of the most enterprising merchants and manufacturers of the time. He was granted, in 1619, a patent of the sole right of making soap in Scotland for twenty-one years. Hitherto foreign soap only had been used, " with the quhilk saipe this kingdome is most shamefullie and mischeantlie abused, the samyn being compoised of suche pestiferous and filthie ingredientis as no civile kingdome, yea even the very rude barbarianis, will nocht allow nor permitt the lyk to be sauld amongis thame[2]." In view of the contemporary reputation of Scotland for dirtiness, it is interesting to read that this " pestiferous and noysome saipe " was said to produce "mony schameful and havie imputationis aganis this kingdome especiallie be strangearis hanting and frequenting this kingdome quha may not abide the stinkin smell of the naiprie and lynning clothes waschin with this filthie saip." Udward's manufacture was not, however, able to supply the whole kingdom, and the restraint on the import of foreign soap was withdrawn in 1624[3]. Udward was also, in 1628, granted a patent for the manufacture of ordnance, the first attempt of that nature in Scotland[4].

[1] *S. P. C. R.*, xiv., p. 558.
[2] *Ibid.*, xii., p. 106.
[3] *Ibid.*, xiii., p. 294.
[4] *Ibid.* (2nd Series), ii., p. 338.

In the same year a patent was granted to two London merchants and one Scot for the sole right of refining sugar in Scotland for thirty-one years, both imported and exported sugar to be free of duty for twenty-one years[1]. The manufacture of glass also received attention. Glass works were set up in 1619, and a Venetian was brought to serve as master[2]. The glass used in Scotland had formerly been brought from Dantzig. A commission was appointed two years later to inquire into the state of the manufacture[3]. They recommended that pieces of glass of each kind manufactured should be brought from England to serve as patterns for the Scots manufacture. The import of foreign glass was forbidden for thirty-one years[4]. In England, Scots glass was the only kind which was allowed to be imported[5].

The ever-active Udward in 1631 obtained a monopoly for the manufacture of salt, for which he had invented a new process[6]. If his invention succeeded in Scotland, he was to be allowed to manufacture it in England and Ireland also. At the same time it was suggested that the amount of salt to be imported into England should be restricted, and also the importation of foreign salt into Scotland. Objections were raised to both proposals. The restraint of the export to England would reduce the quantity produced, and then both coal- and salt-works would be injured, as it did not pay to work the coal unless it could be used in the salt manufacture[7]. Foreign

---

[1] *S. P. C. R.*, xii., p. 91.

[2] *S. P. Domestic, James I*, cxii., 28.

[3] *S. P. C. R.*, xii., p. 428.   [4] *Ibid.*, p. 439.

[5] *S. P. Domestic, James I*, cxxi., 111.

[6] *S. P. C. R.* (2nd Series), iv., p. 213.   [7] *Ibid.*, p. 235.

salt was necessary for the salting of fish, a very important industry, as Scotland exported large quantities of salted fish both to France and Spain.

The condition of the fishing industry was a matter of great concern, especially to Charles I. The fishing on the Scottish coasts was of course a very valuable national asset, but it was far from being developed to the utmost extent. The disturbed state of the Highlands and Islands was a great drawback to fishing in the seas and lochs there. It was said in 1605 that the fishermen were debarred by the "violence and barbarous crueltie, abusis, and extortiouns of the hielandis and cuntremen" from that "maist profitabill and easie fisching[1]." The state of these parts improved a little through James's efforts, but then the Dutch stepped in and took a large share of the fishing. Englishmen also began to fish in Scottish waters. In 1623 the burghs complained of the "heavie hurt the haill borrowis of this realme doth sustain be the Inglishmen and Fleymings who hes laitlie taken upone tred of fishing in the North and West Yles of this kingdome[2]." They were further alarmed by the permission given by Charles in 1627 to the Earl of Seaforth to erect a burgh in Stornoway, which was to be settled with Dutchmen who were to undertake the trade of fishing[3]. This prospective intrusion of the Dutch also aroused English jealousy: "from our fish they ground their stock of all their other adventures and make Holland the Staple for all Christendom, from Scotland they serve France, Germany and all the Countries within the Baltic sea[4]." Scots and English

---

[1] *Royal Burghs*, ii., p. 204.   [2] *Ibid.*, iii., p. 142.

[3] *Ibid.*, pp. 260, 291, 303.

[4] *S. P. Domestic, Charles I*, clii., 69, 70, 71.

both agreed as to the necessity of expelling the Dutch
from Scottish waters, but there the agreement ended.
England wanted to share the benefits of the fishing, while
the Scots were almost as anxious to exclude the English
as the Dutch. A project was made for forming a great
company, with an elaborate organisation, of Scots, English
and Irish, for carrying on the fishing all round the coast.
Charles was much interested in the scheme, and wrote
many letters to the Scottish Privy Council urging them
to further its promotion. One of these ended with the
words: "this is a worke of so great good to both my
kingdomes that I have thought good by these few lines
of my owne hand seriouslie to recommend it unto yow
The furthering of which will ather oblige or disoblige me
more than anie one business that has happened in my
time[1]."

A committee was appointed to consider the whole
question. They found the "associatioun with England
to be verie inconvenient to the estait." The Scots first
of all insisted on the reservation of all the fishing in
the lochs and bays, and within fourteen miles of the
coasts, so that the English would have been in no better
position than they were before the association was formed.
They also raised many difficulties as to the settlements of
the English on the coasts to cure their fish, and as to
their trade with the natives. The negotiations almost
came to grief on the subject of the reservations. Charles
wrote to the Earl of Menteith in 1631: "yow must deall
about the reservations for the fisching busines to keip
these places from being reserved that I have told you
of, becaus I foresee that otherwyse that great business,

[1] *Acts, Scotland*, v., p. 229.

whereof I have had so great a care of, will run a hazard[1]."
In the end the only reservations made were of the fishing
between "St Tabsheid and Ridheid," and the "Mules of
Galloway and Kintyre," that is, of the Firths of Forth and
Clyde. Letters Patent were issued erecting the company[2],
and a charter constituting the association sent down to
Scotland. The government was vested in twelve coun-
cillors, half Scottish, and half English and Irish. To
propitiate the Scots, the charter was drawn up with
"speciall care to preserve the dignitie of that our ancient
kingdome." The company at first seemed to carry on
its work vigorously, especially the English members, who
occasionally complained of their treatment in the Highlands. But the disturbances arising from the Civil War
interrupted this, as many other pursuits, and after the
Restoration it was found to be very much neglected.

The results of the reign of James and of the first part
of that of Charles in Scotland, economically speaking, was
a considerable industrial development, greatly due to the
personal interest of both sovereigns, manifested chiefly
through the action of their Privy Council. But the latter
part of Charles's reign was far from favourable to continued economic prosperity. In spite of the increased
taxation to meet the expense of the army in England
and the devastation caused by Montrose's campaigns, industry and trade were still carried on for a time, though
under ever-increasing difficulties. Cromwell's invasions,
however, devastated the country and dealt a very severe
blow to Scottish economic prosperity, from which it did
not recover for many years.

[1] *Royal Letters*, II., p. 550.
[2] *Acts, Scotland*, v., pp. 239—243.

In 1643 the Privy Council appointed a commission to establish manufactories[1], and in 1645 the Act in favour of manufactories was passed[2]. This Act granted various privileges and exemptions for the benefit of manufacturers, including an exemption from serving with the army or having soldiers quartered on them. It was the first of a series which established a system of parliamentary protection of industry in Scotland, continued after the Restoration, and becoming fully developed by the Act of 1681. The increasing expenses of army maintenance made new taxation necessary, and in 1644 an excise was established. The commodities taxed were ale, beer, wine, aqua vitae, tobacco, cattle, sheep, silk stuffs, cloths and coal, but all the manufactures of the kingdom were exempted[3]. The government shewed its desire as far as possible to encourage, or at all events, not to handicap industry, but doubtless the strain of supporting an army had begun to tell upon the country before the English invasions with their disastrous results alike to industry and commerce laid the country desolate.

b. TRADE WITH ENGLAND. COLONISATION AND TRADE IN AMERICA. COLONISATION IN IRELAND

Trade with England

Scottish trade during this period was carried on along much the same lines as before the Union. Scotland did not gain any share in England's foreign trade. Her merchants still confined themselves to voyages to

---

[1] S. P. C. R., VII., p. 391.   [2] Acts, Scotland, VI., p. 174.
[3] Ibid., VI., p. 75.

France, Spain and the Baltic, and did not venture to join in the East Indian, African or Levant trades. Nor did they share in the Plantation trade which was gradually becoming of great importance to England. Only one Scotsman is mentioned as trading from Scotland to America before 1660, an Aberdeen merchant[1]. Farther north the enterprising Udward began a fishing trade in the Greenland seas, but he met with much opposition from the English companies who traded thither.

In her European trade, which was by far the most important, Scotland suffered from her connection with England throughout the seventeenth century. She became involved in the wars which her sovereign waged as King of England, which handicapped her trade and from which she did not derive any benefits. This was especially the case with France and Holland, with whom she chiefly traded. During these wars her trade with England's enemy was prohibited, though as a matter of fact the prohibitions were not always regarded. She was taxed to support them and had also to maintain herself in a state of defence while they continued, while she reaped no benefit from them in the end. For the support of the Elector Palatine in 1621, £1,200,000 Scots payable in three years was granted to James, "the greatest taxatione that ever was granted in Scotland heirtofoir in aney age." In 1625 a grant of £400,000 was made to Charles for support in his war with France. These additional burdens fell very heavily on the mercantile classes, who were already suffering from the hindrance to their trade caused by the war.

[1] *S. P. Col., Charles I*, ix., 118.

James's desire to make his two kingdoms one was shewn by his union scheme. Although that was a failure, he afterwards did all he could to bring the administration of England and Scotland as near uniformity as possible. His ecclesiastical policy was directed towards the setting up of the same form of Church government in Scotland as in England. Of less importance but more wisdom was his introduction of the English Justice of the Peace system into Scotland. In commercial affairs, he tried to make the laws relating to navigation in Scotland conform to those in England. In 1615 he issued a Proclamation in England enforcing the earlier statutes with regard to navigation. These declared that only English ships should be used in shipping goods to or from English ports[1]. In Scotland this policy had never been followed, but in the same year James suggested that regulations of the same nature should be made there. There was much discussion of the proposal. The chief reason urged against it by the burghs was, that if they should restrain their trade to native ships, other nations would do likewise. This would mean " decay and wrack to our schipping," as a large number of ships were employed by foreigners, and " the half of the number of schippis quhilkis ar presentlie in Scotland will serve for our awin privat tred[2]." The Privy Council were of another opinion. They declared that "the cuntry, quhilk of laite yeiris wes furnist with a nomber of good and strong schippis is now become empty of schipping...whereas yf according to the loveabill custome of

<hr />

[1] *Growth of English Industry and Commerce*, W. Cunningham, ii., p. 210, note ; i., pp. 363, 435.

[2] *Letters and State papers during the reign of James I* (Abbotsford Club), i., p. 243.

all otheris weile governit commonwealthis no strangearis shippis wer sufferit to be frauchtet be the subjectis of this cuntrey quhen Scottis and Inglis schippis may be had the shipping of this cuntrey wald daylie incresce[1]." The skippers were also anxious for the restraint. The Council decided that for the south and east, "France, Flanderis, Spayne and Italie and utheris southe and west pairtis and portis quhair this kingdome hes commerce" the restraint should be made. The freight prices were to be settled by representatives both of the merchants and of the skippers. But it was not found possible to regulate the "easterlyne" trade, as from those parts were brought necessary commodities such as timber, pitch and tar. These the country could not do without, but the native ships were not fitted for carrying them, therefore importation in foreign vessels was still allowed[2]. According to the Proclamation of 1615, the term "native" ships included also English ships. These regulations, however, soon fell into abeyance.

The fact of the Union and the sovereign's anxiety to draw the two nations together seem to have resulted in some increase of the trade between the two countries, though neither nation was at all popular with the other. The English expressed many fears at the time of the Union that herds of impoverished Scots would descend upon them, and, like the lean kine of Egypt, would devour their prosperity. The King did his best to restrain his more needy subjects from following him. "Horners" were forbidden to pass into England[3]. Skippers were forbidden

[1] *S. P. C. R.*, xi., p. 202. *Royal Burghs*, iii., p. 88.
[2] *S. P. C. R.*, xii., p. 107.
[3] *Ibid.*, ix., p. 301.

to take any " beggarlie passengeris" thither[1]. Later a
licence was required for anyone who wished to go to
England[2]. These were only to be granted to " gentlemen
of goode qualitie and merchantis for traffique[3]." James
suited his own convenience in prohibiting one class of
person from repairing to his English court—persons who
came to sue for debts due from the King, " whereas thair is
no sorte of importunitie more ungratious to His Majesty[4]."
A few Englishmen seem to have repaired to Scotland,
artisans, as the tanners who were introduced, and a few
glass workers; also some manufacturers, two who set up
a sugar-refining work, some who had patents for searching
for saltpetre, or for working gold and silver mines, and
others. On the whole, however, there does not seem to
have been much settlement by either nationality in the
country of the other.

The merchants repairing to England were still looked
upon as strangers, whatever their legal position might be.
Those trading to London found it necessary in 1612 to
appoint an agent to look after their interests there, as
they were " wonderfullie abusit be the serchours customers
and others thair[5]." In ports on the east coast—Yarmouth,
Hull, Lynn, etc.—they complained of being made to pay
larger entry and officers' fees than they had formerly paid
in London[6]. Soon after the Proclamation of 1615 the
farmers of the customs in London proposed to search
all Scottish ships coming to that port, which was not done
in any other country and was only suggested " to trouble
his Majesties good subjectis." James took this matter

[1] *S. P. C. R.*, ix., p. 377.   [2] *Ibid.*, x., p. 173.
[3] *Ibid.*, p. 324.   [4] *Ibid.*, p. 408.
[5] *Royal Burghs*, ii., p. 380.   [6] *Ibid.*, p. 462.

into consideration, and after representations from the Scottish Privy Council on the question, he refused to grant permission to search Scots ships[1]. Complaints and disagreements were very common, especially with the Scots merchants, who resorted to England more than English merchants to Scotland. This was the case in particular branches of trade as well as in general commercial relations. In any direction where the interests of the two countries clashed, England was always anxious to regulate Scottish affairs to meet her convenience. She manifested the same spirit as in her dealings with Ireland and with the Plantations. England was to be the head, her interests were to be supreme, and their affairs were to be regulated as best to conduce to her prosperity. England forgot that Scotland was neither a conquered country nor a dependency settled with her own " blood and treasure." And in time she found that there was a strong Scottish national spirit, and that her own interests would be better served by concession than by coercion.

The negotiations regarding the wool trade in James's reign are an illustration of England's attitude. The cloth trade was the most important of the English industries at this period. The supply of raw material was a question of great importance, and the export of wool was forbidden. All through the seventeenth century there was friction between the two countries regarding this trade. England wanted first of all to prevent the Scots from taking English wool to Scotland, and then exporting it to supply the rivals of England ; and also, if possible, to secure that English manufacturers should be able to command the supply of Scots wool also, and that it should not be exported to any

[1] *S. P. C. R.*, xi., p. 343.

other country. For a few years before 1622 there was no
restraint on the wool trade between the two countries,
and during that period there were some complaints of the
export of English wool through Scotland to the continent.
The Merchant Adventurers complained in 1616 that the
Hollanders had prohibited the use of their cloth, and were
promoting their own manufactures. They demanded that
the export of wool from Scotland should be forbidden, as
well as from England[1]. The export from Scotland had
been forbidden at different times, but the prohibitions
were never strictly enforced. In 1622 the export of
English wool to Scotland was prohibited in order that
it might not be supplied to foreign markets by the Scots.
The English authorities then considered that the Scots
wool supply might be reserved exclusively for their use.
Commissioners from both nations were ordered to meet,
"to aduise of the best way, how the Woolles of that Our
Kingdom of Scotland which shall not there be draped
may be brought hither into England...that all parts of
Our Dominion may mutually be helpful one to another,
and further their common good and that our neighbouring
nations may not be furnished with Wools...from any our
Realms or Dominions, and thereby be enabled to hinder
the vent of our Cloth...it being the most staple commodity of this our realme of England[2]." But wool, in
spite of occasional prohibitions, was one of the chief
articles of Scottish trade. The point of view of the
Scots commissioners was therefore different. If "the
vent sould be absolutlie restreaned to Ingland...quhen
Englische salbe assured that we have no privilege to

---

[1] S. P. Domestic, James I, LXXXVIII., 76.
[2] Ibid., CXXXIII., 28.

vent our woollis bot with thame...they will contemne and scorne to give pryces for our Wooll to the countreyis great prejudice[1]." In the end nothing was done, the English commissioners "being maid to understand that the mater wes not of that importance as wes pretendit[2]." Although no definite arrangement was made, a good deal of Scots wool was brought to England, some by land and some by sea. There was a good deal of trade between the two countries by sea, especially in coal, which was brought to London in large quantities. The ports to which the Scots most resorted were London, Bristol, Plymouth, Yarmouth, Newcastle, and also some ports in North Wales. In 1620 the Bristol merchants complained that the owners there were "few and poore in regard of the frequent resort of Scottish shippes hither[3]."

When the Bishops' War broke out in 1639, commercial intercourse with England was stopped, and Scottish trade suffered considerably. All Scottish ships in English ports were arrested[4], and others were taken which were sailing to foreign ports. In 1640 over fifty Scots ships were detained in various English harbours, besides several in Ireland[5]. These were all released on the conclusion of peace. The English were said to have suffered more than the Scots from the stoppage of trade, especially from a dearth of coal, of which large quantities were usually brought from Scotland to London and other English towns. After the peace in 1640, there was no prohibition of trade until the English invasion in 1650. The

[1] *S. P. C. R.*, xiii., p. 175.　　[2] *Ibid.*, p. 233.
[3] *S. P. Domestic, James I*, cxiii., 23.
[4] *Ibid., Charles I*, ccccLxix., 87.
[5] *Ibid.*, ccccLxvii., 126.

royalist privateers and pirates were, however, a great
hindrance to trade in spite of the Commonwealth fleet.
They infested the coasts, and even made it difficult for
the Scots to victual their forces in England. In 1644,
on the representation of the Scots commissioners, eight
ships were appointed to guard the Scottish coasts, but
they do not seem to have been of much service. Communication with France and Holland was much hindered,
"to the utter ruine of many merchants." The burghs
suffered so much that in 1644 a grant was made to them
of £15,000 to compensate them for their losses by sea
and land, and in 1647 another grant of £20,000[1]. The
trading estate as a whole, though fairly prosperous during
the early years of the seventeenth century, yet suffered
considerably during the decade 1640 to 1650, and was
in no condition to support the losses incurred during the
English invasions and occupation.

Of the resentment of the English merchants at any
infringement of their privileges on the part of the Scots,
there is, during this period, an instance in the Greenland
trade. The ubiquitous Udward, in 1627, obtained from
Charles, under the Great Seal of Scotland, a patent to
trade and make oil by fishing in Greenland and in the
islands adjoining[2]. The oil was to be used in the soap-
works which had been set up in 1619. The English
Muscovy Company, which had the monopoly in England
of trading thither, attacked the two ships which were sent
out, forcibly preventing them from taking any share in
the fishing[3]. They declared that the Scottish patent was

[1] *Acts, Scotland*, VI., Part I., pp. 226, 797.
[2] *Register of Royal Letters* (Earl of Stirling), I., p. 150.
[3] *S. P. Domestic, Charles I*, DXL., 74.

not in force in England, and that the Scots were merely interlopers. In 1630 matters were further complicated, for two Englishmen, one who had formerly belonged to the Muscovy Company and another, " an adwersary to the Company," made preparations for trading from Yarmouth under the Scots patent[1]. The intrusion of English interlopers still further alarmed the English company, and they resisted the ships which sailed under cover of the Scots patent with "wild outrages, ryotts, Murther and effusion of blood." The Scottish Privy Council, aroused by the slight to the powers of the Scottish Crown, remonstrated against its liberties and privileges being "trod underfoot." It was declared that "the question now standeth between the two nations," and urged that a committee of both should be nominated to settle the matter[2]. This was agreed to, and several well-known men were appointed on both sides : the Lord Privy Seal, the Lord Marshal, and Secretaries Coke and Windebank for England ; the Earls of Stirling, Roxburgh and others for Scotland[3]. The committee seem to have agreed that the holder of the Scots patent should be allowed to bring a certain quantity of oil from Greenland to Scotland, for the use of the Scottish soap manufacturers only. About this time Udward transferred his patent to a certain Thomas Horth, who carried on the trade for some time, although he also had some disagreement later with the English companies.

[1] *S. P. Domestic, Charles I*, cxci., 21.
[2] *Ibid.*, cclxxxii., 37.   [3] *Ibid.*, cclxxxiv., 67.

Colonisation and Trade in America

Although the Scottish nation as a whole was not at
this time imbued with the trading and colonising spirit,
there were some few individuals of the type of Raleigh
and the Gilberts who were anxious that the Scots should
have some interest in the New World. The best known
of these was Sir William Alexander, Earl of Stirling, poet,
statesman, courtier, adventurer. He, in 1621, sought and
received a grant of the land between Newfoundland and
New England, to be held of his Majesty from his kingdom
of Scotland[1]. The land was given the name of New
Scotland. James took a great interest in the scheme
of plantation, and suggested for its encouragement that
a certain number of baronetcies should be created, to be
granted to the larger settlers[2], as had been done in the
Ulster plantation. Each baronet was to have a grant of
30,000 acres, on which he was either to establish six
settlers or to pay 2000 marks[3]. It was considered a "fitt
and convenient means of disburding this His Majesties
said ancient kingdome of all such younger brether and
meane gentlemen quhois moyens ar short of their birth
worth or myndis." The promoters also hoped that the
settlement would prove advantageous to Scottish trade.
But there was no eagerness to join in the project, which
seems strange considering the number of Scotsmen who
flocked to join foreign armies. About a hundred and ten
baronets were created, of whom twelve were English, but
a number of these were made after the settlement had

[1] *S. P. C. R.*, xii., p. 550.   [2] *Ibid.*, p. 616.
[3] *Ibid.*, pp. 649, 721.

been given up, and few, if any, took any practical interest in the scheme.

The first settlers were sent out by Alexander in 1622[1]. They spent the winter in Newfoundland, surveyed the coast of Nova Scotia, and returned home next year[2]. Later another detachment of settlers went out, and in 1627 two ships, one from London and the other from Dumbarton, sailed with powder, ordnance, etc. for their use[3]. Next year Alexander's son joined the colonists with four ships, returning to Scotland in 1628, leaving seventy men and two women in Nova Scotia[4]." The sole right of trading in the "Gulf and River of Canada," for beaver skins, furs and hides, was granted to the two Alexanders, father and son. Connection with the English settlements was to be encouraged. In 1631 licence, under the Scottish seal, was given to William Clayborne, one of the Council in Virginia, to "keep a course for interchange of trade" with Nova Scotia and New England[5]. Unfortunately the situation of the Scottish colony was ill-chosen. In 1603 a settlement had been made by the French, and New Scotland was situated in the territory which they considered they had taken possession of as Acadia and New France. Port Royal was the headquarters of their settlement. In 1613 an Englishman, Captain Argall, took

---

[1] *Register of Royal Letters*, i., p. 120.

[2] *Annals*, Sir James Balfour, ii., p. 310.

[3] *Royal Letters*, i., p. 145.   [4] *Ibid.*, p. xxvii.

[5] *Ibid.*, ii., p. 527. In 1638 complaints were made that Clayborne, "by vertue of a Commission under His Majesty's hand and seal," made two settlements in Chesapeake Bay, on territory claimed by Lord Baltimore. It was decided that the land was included in Baltimore's patent, and moreover that Clayborne's commission was "only a Lycense under the Signett of Scotland to trade with the Indians." *Maryland Archives*, iii., p. 73.

possession of the fort there and dislodged the French[1]. No English settlement was made, however, and the Scots found neither French nor English colony when their small band of settlers went out. They also established themselves at Port Royal. In 1630, however, on the conclusion of peace between England and France, the latter claimed Nova Scotia by virtue of the settlement of 1603[2]. The Scots urged that the French had given up their settlement at Port Royal, and had never laid claim to the land since the Scots charter had been granted. Also they had settled before the outbreak of the war[3]. Charles hesitated to give up the claims of his Scots subjects, but in 1632, by the treaty of St Germain-en-Laye, it was provided that Port Royal should be abandoned[4]. Quebec, which had been gained by the English, was also given up. Nova Scotia was taken by the English again in 1656, and the Alexander family asserted their claim to it, but without success. It was again given up to France by the peace of 1667.

Scotland was unfortunate in her seventeenth century colonising attempts. Nova Scotia was in French, Darien in Spanish territory, and both had to be given up. But the "thoughts of the nation were not yet turned to trade," and there was no national remonstrance when the earlier settlement was abandoned. Nor were there present any of the peculiarly aggravating circumstances of the Darien episode. Charles was genuinely interested in this Scottish scheme, and did his best to maintain it. William, though certainly driven by necessity, acted with callousness. But, had Scotland been able to maintain her settlement in

[1] *Royal Letters*, I., p. 97.   [2] *S. P. C. R.*, III., p. 614.
[3] *S. P. Col.*, V., 102. II.   [4] *Royal Letters*, I., pp. 68, 74.

Nova Scotia, she might have found an outlet for her
energies and a market for her goods, and much of the
bitterness of the latter part of the century might have
been avoided.

One or two other commercial schemes are recorded
in the manuscripts of the period, grandiose and vague in
theory, and never put into execution in practice. In 1633
Charles wrote informing the Lord Advocate that the Earl
of Stirling, Sir John Hay and others were going to form
a society for trade. He was ordered to grant a warrant
to them of power to form companies of any who would
undertake any "new traffique in America Asia Africa and
Muscovie not formerlie used in that Kingdome[1]." In the
next year a patent was drawn up giving thirty-one years'
monopoly of the trade in Africa, between the Senegal
River and the Cape of Good Hope, to certain persons
unnamed[2]. It does not seem, however, that any advantage was taken of these powers. Only one merchant
had sufficient enterprise to establish a trade to America
from Scotland, one John Burnett of Aberdeen. He was
"the sole Merchant of our Kingdom of Scotland, that hath
supplyed the plantacon of that our Colony of Virginia and
become our tenant there." In 1637, orders were given
that all tobacco from Virginia should be brought to
London. Burnett feared that he was included in the
order, but Charles in the next year wrote to the Governor
and Council of Virginia, declaring that it was "noewayes
intended to impeach the freedome of comerce and Traffique
into our Kingdom of Scotland by the Natives thereof,"
and that Burnett was to have "free comerce and Traffique
from our Kingdome of Scotlande to that our Colony and

[1] *Royal Letters*, ii., p. 702.   [2] *Ibid.*, i., p. 160

from thence back again[1]." Unfortunately Charles's liberal
policy in this respect was not followed by the Parliaments
of his son.

Colonisation in Ireland

Though unsuccessful in their American colony one
settlement of great importance was made by the Scots
during James's reign. This was the plantation of Ulster,
which not only modified the whole character of the North
of Ireland, but contributed later numbers of sturdy Scots-
Irish to the building up of the American colonies. The
rebellion of Sir Cahir O'Dogherty in 1608 and its punish-
ment made an opportunity for planting a colony in Ulster,
as had been attempted in the previous reign in Ulster and
Munster. In the first scheme for this plantation 90,000
acres were set aside for which the Scots might apply, and
this was quickly taken up by seventy-seven would-be
settlers. Finally the scheme was revised by the English
Privy Council, and 81,000 acres in Donegal, Tyrone and
Fermanagh were distributed amongst fifty-nine Scottish
undertakers[2]. They had each to give security that they
would fulfil certain conditions, build a substantial fortified
house or castle and establish a certain number of settlers,
differing according to the size of the estate. The Earl
of Abercorn, Lord Ochiltree and other well-known names
were amongst the list of undertakers. They took over a
number of men, and also cattle, sheep, etc. for stocking
the land. The traffic between the north of Ireland and
the west of Scotland became so great that the passage
became a constant ferry. The boatmen and skippers saw

[1] *S. P. Col.*, ix., 118.   [2] *S. P. C. R.*, ix., p. lxxvi.

their advantage here and raised prices to "ane extra-ordinarie heicht[1]," but after some complaints the Justices of the Peace on the west coast were directed to fix the rates of freight and passage. Great care was taken to prevent undesirable persons from crossing over, and also to prevent the passage of stolen goods. Every person had to have a licence before he could be received on any ship, and traffic with Ireland was only allowed at certain ports. These were Corshorne, Portpatrick, Kirkcudbright, Ballintrae, Ayr, Irvine, Largs, Dumbarton and Glasgow[2]. At these there was much traffic, first of all in carrying over the settlers and their effects, and later in trade between the colony and the south and west of Scotland. The settlers were very successful, and became a hard-working and prosperous agricultural community. A great deal of their produce seems to have found a market in Scotland— butter, eggs and cheese especially were imported—and the Irish trade became one of great importance to the ports on the Clyde and the south-west coasts.

c. Trade with France, Holland, etc.

The beginning of the Scottish breach with France was made in the sixteenth century, when in 1560 the Scots accepted the Reformed Religion. The breach was widened with the union of the crowns of England and Scotland in 1603. The bonds of union—a common sovereign and a common Protestantism—were more obvious than the seeds of dissension—different forms of Protestantism, different Parliaments and different commercial interests. The Scots, conscious of the last, held firmly to their trading privileges

[1] *S. P. C. R.*, IX., p. 478.   [2] *Ibid.*, X., p. 566.

in France, which were retained during the first part of the seventeenth century, although not without frequent applications for renewal. But the old friendly feeling and continual intercourse were quickly becoming things of the past. The English connection brought with it also more active disabilities, arising from English wars with France, in which Scotland was an unwilling participator, and from the danger that Scotland would be included in the retaliations caused by English policy.

As early as 1614, a difficulty of this nature arose. In reply to the English Proclamation of that year, prohibiting any goods from being imported into England except in English ships, the French king issued an edict to the same effect for France, " to the grate preuidice of the merchant estait of the kingdome of Scotland." The Scots factors at once complained to the Parliament of Paris, pointing out that the French still had liberty of trading in Scotland, in spite of the English regulations. The French decision was that the edict "did no wayes extend towards the subiects of the Kingdome of Scotland, their ancient friends and allayes," and that the Scots were still as free within the dominions of France as they had ever been[1]. The year before, the Scots privileges in Normandy had again been ratified[2]. Scotland's next alarm was that her merchants might be involved in the difficulties of Louis XIII's Huguenot subjects, because they were also of the Reformed Religion. They urged the King to order his ambassador in Paris to ask Louis to continue the Scots privileges. The French king promised to do so, " for the love he carried to the Scotts nation the most ancient allayes of the French crown[3]."

[1] *Annals*, II., p. 58.   [2] *Royal Burghs*, II., pp. 576—580.
[3] *Annals*, II., p. 83.

The wars with Spain and France which broke out in 1625 and 1627 were serious checks to Scottish as to English trade. For a few months in 1626 no ship-owners were allowed to undertake any voyage, except with licence of the Privy Council, as his Majesty might require some of the vessels to serve in the fleet[1]. The import of wine from France was also forbidden, except in Scots bottoms. Both the Scottish and English ships which sailed to Bordeaux and other ports at the vintage time in the next year were arrested. The Scottish ships were, however, released in a short time because of their ancient league[2]. In the same year no offers were made for the farm of the impost on wines when it was rouped. This was chiefly accounted for by the interruption of trade with France[3]. Shortly after this the import of French goods was forbidden altogether. This was followed by remonstrances from the merchants. They declared that they now had to take the native commodities, which they usually disposed of in France, to the Low Countries. If they were not allowed to get French goods there, their trade would be ruined, for they already got a sufficiency of the products of the Low Countries[4]. Trade would then decay, for the " Easterlynne trade being in these difficult tymes interrupted and in a manner relinquished," there would be no vent for their commodities, and they would remain on the merchants' hands. Later they complained that English merchants were allowed to import French wines from the Low Countries to England, and the merchants begged his Majesty " to vouchsafe the lyke princelie in-

[1] *S. P. C. R.* (2nd Series), I., pp. 431, 445.
[2] *Annals*, II., p. 158.   [3] *S. P. C. R.*, II., p. 567.
[4] *Ibid.*, pp. 243, 244.

dulgence to your subjects of this Kingdome." In 1629, in view of his Majesty's visit to Scotland, the prohibition on the import of French wines was at last discharged.

In 1635, by an arrest of the "gritt counsall of the estait of France," the Scots merchants were exempted from some new duties imposed in Normandy[1]. When the Bishops' War began in 1639, there was some alarm in England because it was rumoured that the French were sending help to the Scots "to foment our disorders for their own interests." It was said too that they were laying heavy burdens on English merchants and favouring the Scots "after the old manner[2]." In spite of this report, the Privy Council wrote to complain to Charles, in 1642, of "the sufferings and losses of our subjects by the infringement of those ancient priviledges and liberties" which they had formerly enjoyed in France. The Council was authorised to send some one to France to endeavour to have the privileges renewed[3], and the Earl of Lothian was dispatched. He seems to have been successful in his mission. Although the Scots retained their privileged position in France during this period, it was not without some effort, and the connection was not so close as it had been during the last two or three centuries. Nevertheless enough of the old tie remained to alarm the English when, as during the Bishops' War, they feared that France would encourage the Scots; and still more when, later in the century, they began to look upon France as their principal rival, both commercially and politically.

During this period England and the Netherlands were

[1] *Royal Burghs*, II., pp. 576—580.

[2] *S. P. Domestic, Charles I*, ccccxx., 32, 120.

[3] *S. P. C. R.*, VII., p. 332.

at peace, and accordingly Scottish trade with the Netherlands was carried on without much interruption. The war
with Spain, however, put a check for a time to almost all
Scottish trade, because of the danger from Spanish ships
of war and from privateers sent out from Dunkirk[1]. These
were such a menace to Scots shipping that the merchants
dare not put to sea at all for a time. Charles sent some
ships to defend the coasts, but as they declined to leave
the harbours they were not of much use as convoys.
On the whole, the merchants who traded to Campvere
flourished and formed there a community of some importance. They were "attached to the true Principles
of Liberty," and are said to have furnished the supporters
of the same principles with arms and ammunition "to
an immense Value." But after the King's death these
merchants, in common with the Scottish nation, lent their
support to the restoration of the monarchy[2].

Spanish trade was of course interrupted by the war
of 1625–32. Even earlier, the Scots merchants trading
thither had some trouble. They had bought a number
of Flemish ships, and these, during the war of Spain
with the Low Countries, were arrested and confiscated
when they reached Spanish ports. The skippers therefore
begged the Council to certify that they were the lawful
owners of the ships which they had bought[3].

In the Portugal trade the merchants complained of
an Englishman, consul at Lisbon, who exacted the same
duties from the Scots ships trading thither as from the

[1] *S. P. C. R.*, xiv., xl., xlv.
[2] *Scottish Staple at Veere*, Davidson and Gray, p. 209.
[3] *S. P. C. R.*, xiii., p. 62.

English, and then did nothing to guard their interests.
The Burghs therefore appointed a consul of their own,
a Scot residing in Lisbon, granting him a duty of a ducat
from every Scottish ship coming to Lisbon[1].

The Baltic trade was important and flourishing. It
was said to be a very necessary trade[2], and was carried on
partly in foreign ships. The imports from the east were
more numerous than the exports thence, for the merchants
declared that "the said trade cannot be, nor never wes
interteyned with the native commodityis of the countrey,
bot that of necessitie some moneyis must be exportit to
that effect[3]." The exports were chiefly skins, woollen cloths
and stockings.

But more numerous than the Scots who traded to
Germany were those who settled there and traded in
the country, mostly as pedlars. Dr Fischer says, "There
was a very large Scottish immigration to Danzig, Königsberg and Poland from the end of the fifteenth Century
and earlier, gradually increasing until the end of the
eighteenth[4]." The traveller Lithgow in 1640 called Poland
the "mother and nurse of the youths and younglings of
Scotland, clothing, feeding and enriching them with the
fatness of her best things, besides 30,000 Scots families
that live incorporate in her bowels[5]." The Scots pedlars
and small merchants were not welcomed by the burghers
either in Poland or Germany, and to defend themselves
they were banded together in Brotherhoods in both

---

[1] *Royal Burghs*, II., p. 280.
[2] Above, p. 35.   [3] *S. P. C. R.*, XIII., p. 120.
[4] *The Scots in Germany*, Th. A. Fischer, p. 31.
[5] *Ibid.*, p. 32.

countries[1]. Some who settled in the large towns were admitted to the number of the citizens. Charles II thought it worth while to try to get financial support from the Scots in Poland, desiring that the King should not permit any to "enjoy the libertie they have in that kingdome but such as shall approve their loyaltie and good affection to us by some supply of money[2]."

The Swedish trade increased considerably in the seventeenth century, Stockholm being the favourite port. In 1636 there were sixteen Scots ships employed in importing salt to Sweden[3].

The Scots, although they had not taken up with any enthusiasm the project of settling in America, left their native country in great numbers for the Continent. Thousands went to serve in the Thirty Years' War, where Leslie and many other warriors of the Civil War served their apprenticeship. Mackay's regiment, 4000 strong in 1626, a detachment of 6000 in 1631, and many others, joined Gustavus Adolphus; and there were many Scots fighting on the other side[4]. A number also took up service in Russia. In 1632 Charles solicited permission for one James Wallace and his servants to pass freely through Denmark, Sweden and Russia, as he was appointed a messenger for conveying letters to and from the Scottish subjects in the service of the Russian Emperor[5]. The military spirit was more active in Scotland during this time than the trading spirit. Religious affairs also became more and more absorbing. The Scottish trading interest,

---

[1] *The Scots in Germany*, Th. A. Fischer, pp. 39, 40.
[2] *H. M. C. R. Portland Papers*, II., pp. 25, 26.
[3] *Scots in Sweden*, Th. A. Fischer, pp. 39, 40.
[4] *History of Scotland*, Hill Burton, VI., p. 118.
[5] *Royal Letters*, II., p. 632.

before the Civil War began, were a fairly prosperous community, but they carried on their trade along the same
lines and in the same manner as their forefathers, almost
untouched by the influences which had effected such
changes in English trade in the sixteenth and early
seventeenth centuries.

Note.—The blank in the Burgh Records from 1631 to 1649 deprives
us of a very important source of information on the commercial and
industrial history of these years.

CHAPTER III

AFTER the King's death, Scotland felt the direct effects of the Civil War more heavily than during the years before. The absence of many of her population with the army in England, and the heavy taxation for their support, had doubtless interrupted industry, and the privateers upon the coasts had greatly hindered trade. But Montrose's campaigns had, for the most part, only affected the northern part of the kingdom, and it was Cromwell's invading army and the Scots resisting force which, in 1650 and 1651, effectually laid waste the country, and caused the dislocation of all industry and trade. In July 1650 Cromwell entered Scotland, and remained there, subduing all the country south of the Forth, until July 1651, when he followed Charles II and the Scottish army south to Worcester. Scotland was then practically conquered, and a body of English commissioners were sent to administer affairs. Steps toward an entire union were taken, and in 1654 the Council of State passed the "Ordinance of Union," which made provision for England and Scotland becoming one Commonwealth, with one Parliament, to which Scotland was to send thirty members. Parliamentary union was accompanied by commercial

union. Trade between the two countries was freed from
all restrictions, as James had endeavoured to secure, and
further, all restraints of exports or imports, all tariffs
and customs were made the same for both countries. The
countries were therefore united for six years as closely as
they were after the final Union of 1707. The conditions
were, however, very different. Scotland in 1654 was a conquered country, and the union was proposed by England,
and its terms drawn up and enforced by an English government. On these grounds it was resented by Scottish
national feeling, but it was also economically unsuccessful.
A devastated and wasted country, weighed down by heavy
taxation, could not within the short space of six years
adapt itself to new trade regulations and tariffs. The old
courses were blocked, there was not sufficient recuperative
power nor encouragement to turn into new channels, and
so Scotland remained inactive and poverty stricken.

The country in the south was laid waste by the Scots
before the battle of Dunbar, and all the Lowlands by the
English forces after their victory. Nicoll, a diarist of
the period, writes: " so, to end this yeir of God 1650,
this Kingdome was for the moist pairte spoyled and over-
run with the enymie, evin from Berwik to the toun of
Air, their being Inglische garisounes in all quarteris
of these boundis, and land murning, languisching and
fading, and left desolat[1]." In the next year, he says:
" this pure land was brocht to oppin confusioun and
schame, the Inglische airmey ramping throw the kingdome without oppositioun destroying our cornes, and
raising money qubairevir they went for maintenance of

[1] *Diary of public transactions* (1649–1666), John Nicoll (Bannatyne
Club), p. 40.

thair airmy and garisoune[1]." Glencairne's rising and
Monk's expedition against him still further laid waste
the land. Monk said that the people were £200,000
poorer by this rebellion, "because of the greate destruc-
tion and waste made by the Enemy, and of what wee
found necessary to destroy that they might be deprived
of sustenance[2]." Complaints regarding the poverty of
the country continue throughout this period. Baillie, a
well-known Presbyterian minister in Glasgow, wrote in
1656: "deep poverty keeps all ranks exceedingly under;
the taxes of all kinds are so great, and trade so little, that
it is a marvel if extreme scarcity of money end not, ere
long, in some mischief[3]." Later it was said that: "povertie
and skaircetie of money daylie increst be ressoun of the
great burdingis and chargis imposit upone the pepill,
quhilk...constraynit thame to sell...evin their household
geirs, insicht and plenisching, and sum thair cloathes[4]."
Cromwell himself bore witness to the condition of the
country: "I do think the Scotch nation have been under
as great a suffering, in point of livelihood and subsistence
outwardly as any people I have yet named to you. I do
think truly they are a very ruined nation[5]." There are
many more accounts of a like nature, continuing until the
Restoration and also for some time after it. The country
took many years to recover from the effects of this period
of civil war and Cromwellian rule.

[1] Nicoll, p. 122.

[2] *Scotland and the Protectorate*, C. H. Firth (Scottish History Society),
p. 212.

[3] *Baillie's Letters and Journals* (Bannatyne Club), iii., p. 357.

[4] Nicoll, p. 207 (1657).

[5] *Cromwell's Letters and Speeches*, Carlyle, ii., pp. 638—639 (1658).

The burden which pressed most severely upon the country was the very heavy taxation imposed to support the English government and garrison, far heavier than had ever been raised before. In 1652 a general assessment of £10,000 a month was levied on Scotland, from which abatements of £2000 or under might be made in districts which had suffered by the war. This was to be based on valuations made in 1629, 1644–5 and 1649[1]. In ascertaining the assessment, Scotland was to be considered "as well in its integrity and intrinsic value before the late wars, as in its present poverty through devastation and spoil by the wars[2]." It never seems to have been possible to raise the whole of the sum, and after Glencairne's rising Monk declared that he could not raise more than £7300 a month[3]. The assessment was not fairly made, for Scotland, in proportion to her resources, was more heavily taxed than England. Of this Monk complained, writing to Secretary Thurloe in 1657 about a new assessment to be levied on the three kingdoms: "I must desire you will consider this poore country which truely I can make itt appeare that one way or other they pay one hundred pounds out of fower for their assessment...and unlesse there be some course taken, that they may come in equality with England, itt will goe hard with this people....And since wee have united them into one Commonwealth, I thinke itt will bee most equall to bring them into an equality[4]." As a result of this and other remonstrances from Monk, the assessment

[1] *Scotland and the Commonwealth*, C. H. Firth (Scottish History Society), p. xxx.

[2] *S. P. Domestic, Interregnum*, cxxxviii., 60—62.

[3] *Scotland and the Protectorate*, p. 95.

[4] *Thurloe State Papers*, vi., p. 330.

in Scotland was fixed at £6000 in 1657, and this amount
continued to be levied till the Restoration. This was also
much heavier than had ever before been raised in Scotland,
and there were numerous complaints against it.

In spite of this heavy taxation, Scotland was far from
being self-supporting. In 1654, the total expenses of the
troops and garrisons in Scotland were £41,235 monthly.
At that time only £4000 monthly could be raised because
of the "broken condition of the country," so that £37,000
had to be supplied from the English Exchequer[1]. In
1659 a statement was made to Parliament by a Committee for inspecting the Treasuries. This shews not
only the national bankruptcy which contributed to the
ruin of the Protectorate government, but also the share
of Scotland in creating the deficit. The debt to the forces
in Scotland was £93,827. 13s. 0¾d., and to the citadel at
Leith £1800. The annual issue for the pay of the same
forces was £270,643. 4s. 2d., and Scotland only contributed
£135,835 to the income of the three kingdoms. The annual
deficit therefore amounted to £134,808. 4s. 2d., without
reckoning the debt, or contributing anything towards the
navy or civil list expenses. The deficit in the total revenues of the three kingdoms was £1,468,098. 12s. 2½d.[2]
Scotland's incorporation was certainly of no financial value
to England, and this knowledge was probably a principal
reason on the English side for the separation of the two
countries in all but name after the Restoration.

The remainder of the revenue was raised from the
Excise and Customs. These were not made to conform

----

[1] An Estimate of the monthly charge in Scotland. *Acts, Scotland,*
vi., Part 2, p. 888.

[2] *Commons Journals,* vii., p. 160.

to the English rates until 1655[1]. Monk anticipated that
there would be some trouble in raising the new excise.
" I intreate your Lordship to spaire us another regiment
of Horse...for the Excise being to bee set on foote here,
people may be a little troublesome Uppon that occasion[2]."
The excise was farmed at £2481 monthly for the first
four months of its existence[3], but afterwards increased,
and in 1659 amounted to £47,444. 13s. 4d.[4] The method
of collecting both excise and customs was reformed, not,
apparently, without need. Thomas Tucker, an English
revenue official, who visited Scotland in 1656 and drew
up an interesting report as to the state of the trade, etc.,
said that " untill of late...there was nothing either of
method or forme discovered in any of them " (i.e. in
either the customs or the excise). "The Collectors received
very uncertainly....The masters of ships, neither Inwards
nor Outwards, were called upon to declare any contents
of theyr vessells...noe goods were ever weighed at landing,
little notice was taken of what was shipped out." Each
collector " pursued his owne way," a way which produced
more for himself than for the State. This branch of the
revenue seems to have increased somewhat during this
period, which was partly no doubt to be attributed to
the better method of collection, and partly also to the
increase in the customs rates, due to the adoption of
English tariffs. This was complained of by the Convention of the Royal Burghs, who sent a copy of the
old book of rates to London to be compared with the new,
in order that " the vast difference betwixt the two being

---

[1] *Acts, Scotland*, VI., Part II., p. 827.
[2] *Scotland and the Protectorate*, p. 260.   [3] *Ibid.*, p. 371.
[4] *Acts, Scotland*, VI., Part II., p. 888.

sein and considderit...the great prejudice the estait of
burrowis with this natione may susteine thairthrow may
be represented to his Hienis the Lord Protector[1]."

Another grievance of the same nature was the prohibition of the export of certain raw materials, especially
wool, hides and skins[2]. These restraints were made in
the interests of English industries. They were able to
use their own raw materials in manufactures, and so
prohibited their export. But the Scots manufactures
had never been able to use all the raw material of the
country. At this time too, their industries had been
interrupted and sometimes ruined by the wars, and there
was no money in the country with which to set up new
manufactures. The export of wool, hides, etc. had also
been a great part of their foreign trade. England was
at last able to make use of the Scottish wool supply, as
she had tried to do under James VI. The government
in Scotland were often urged by the English authorities
to encourage and establish manufactures. As the Burghs
pointed out, however, this could not be done without
money; money came by trade, and there could be little
trade as long as the export of their principal commodities
was prohibited. The Commissioners " considderit ane act
...dischairging the exportatione of skin wooll hyd and
utheris suche commodities...and ordaining the samyne to
be maid use of at home in manufactories to be erected for
that effect...and withall consideddering the low conditione of
this natione...and that the exportatione of thes commodities wes the onlie means quhairby their tread subsisted
in the natione and forrane commodities and money imported without the which they ar altogether unable for

[1] *Royal Burghs*, III., p. 397 (1655).   [2] *Ibid.*, p. 393.

erecting of the manufactories[1]." The difficulty was that
if the two countries were to be completely united, there
could not be different restraints for each. Scottish industries were not as well developed as English, and her
principal exports were raw materials, whereas English
exports were chiefly manufactures. Therefore, as the
regulations for export were made in English interests,
they pressed hardly upon the Scots. Nor was this the
time when Scotland could be forced to become a manufacturing country, for she was a conquered country with
exhausted resources. It was not until after the Restoration
that she began to encourage and develop manufactures,
and not until these had made some progress was she
really convinced of the necessity for an incorporating
union with England.

By freedom of trade with England in one commodity,
salt, the Scots were the gainers. There had for some
time been an import of Scottish salt into England. About
1637 it was agreed that the import of Scots salt into
England should be restricted to 8000 wey yearly[2], but
this restriction does not seem to have lasted very long.
The duty on Scots salt was higher than that on English,
but not so much as that on foreign salt. The manufacturers complained of the Scottish competition, and in
1647 the duty on English salt was removed altogether[3].
The manufacturers, however, were not satisfied, and in
1649 Scots salt was made to pay as much as foreign salt,
i.e. three half-pence per gallon[4]. But at the same time,

---

[1] *Royal Burghs*, III., p. 391 (1654).

[2] *S. P. Domestic, Charles I*, CCCLXXVII., 27.

[3] *Growth of English Industry and Commerce*, W. Cunningham, II.,
p. 309.

[4] *S. P. Domestic, Charles II*, CCXXXIV., 197.

an excise of one half-penny per gallon was levied on English salt. The result was that "the Scottish salt undermined the English," and a hundred and sixty salt-works had to be given up. The salt-workers, we are told, hoped for some relief when the Rump Parliament was dissolved by Cromwell, but "met with the quite contrary," for by the Union of 1654 Scots salt could pass into England without paying any duty at all[1]. The salt-makers in the north of England at once declared that their industry would be totally ruined. Salt, they said, could be made much more cheaply in Scotland, as the people there could be paid in kind instead of in money[2]. In a debate in Parliament on the Union in 1656, it was urged that some extra excise should be placed on Scots salt, to save the Newcastle salt-works from ruin. But no tax was imposed, for three reasons. Firstly, that for three years already there had been free trade in salt, and the English works had not suffered. Secondly, for the statesmanlike reason that "if you make an union you must allow them as much priviledge as your selves, and be as much concerned for their good and advantage as your selves." And also because salt from Scotland might make Newcastle salt cheaper, which would be "a generall good to the Nation and a generall good is to be preferred before a particular," an interesting assertion for the period from the point of view of economic theory[3]. The import of cheap Scots salt did as a matter of fact injure the English makers, for about this time some eighty salt-works

[1] Jno. Collins, *Salt and Fishery* (1682).
[2] *S. P. Domestic, Interregnum*, XCII., 231 ; XCIV., 68.
[3] *Cromwellian Union*, C. S. Terry (Scottish History Society), p. lxx.

in the north had to be shut down[1]. A little later, it was
the turn of the Scots to complain. Their troubles arose
from the connection of the salt manufacture with the
coal-works. These produced two kinds of coal, great and
small. The former were as a rule exported, and the latter
employed in the salt-works. But if anything hindered the
sale of the great coals, no small were produced, and the salt
manufacture was then at a standstill. Now in 1656, a
duty of 4*s.* per ton was imposed on great coal exported
in British ships, and 8*s.* on coal exported in foreign ships[2].
Both coal and salt owners complained, declaring that "the
trade of Coales and Salt (the best staple commodityes of
this Nation) must be utterly ruined[3]." The "intrinsick
value" of the coal, they said, was only 4*s.* per ton. English
coal could more easily bear the tax than Scottish, as a
great deal of the Newcastle coal was used in England,
and was therefore not liable to the tax. Also the Dutch
found English coal indispensable in their iron-works, but
Scottish coal was only used in the Netherlands for soap-
works and brewing, and was not absolutely necessary.
Indeed coal from Luyck was already being substituted
for it[4]. It was to the Netherlands, too, that most of
the Scottish coal was sent. Twenty thousand people
were said to be affected by a decline in the prosperity
of the coal- and salt-works, while the revenue would
suffer greatly from the loss of the customs on these
two commodities. After these remonstrances, the duty
was temporarily reduced in 1658 to 2*s.* 6*d.* and 5*s.* per ton[5],

---

[1] Jno. Collins, *Salt and Fishery* (1682).

[2] Scobell, *Acts*, Part II., p. 387.

[3] *S. P. Domestic, Commonwealth*, clxxix., 65.

[4] *Ibid.*, 65 ; clxxx., 12, 12. i.

[5] *S. P. Domestic, Interregnum*, lxxviii., 783—785.

but seems to have been increased again, for in 1660 the Burghs asked that the "extraordinarie imposition upon coall and salt may be moderated." The advantage of the Scottish over the English salt-works was therefore only temporary.

There does not seem to have been much increase in the amount of trade with England, in spite of freedom from restraint. The principal commodities brought from Scotland were, as before, coal, salt, plaiding, linen, hides and some wool. In addition, efforts were made to secure supplies of masts from the north of Scotland, because the trade with the Baltic had been interrupted by the Navigation Act. Several persons were sent north at different times to get masts, and to examine the state of the forests, but the timber was probably not sufficiently well-grown, and Scotland did not become a source of supply. During the Dutch and Spanish wars, the trade increased. While the war with Spain (1656–8) was going on, nearly all Scots ships confined their trade to English ports, finding it unsafe to venture further.

Little trade to the plantations in America was carried on as yet. Tucker, in his Report, says that some from Glasgow had ventured as far as Barbadoes, but they sustained such losses from coming back late in the year that the trade had been given up.

Foreign trade did not, on the whole, prosper under Commonwealth and Protectorate government. The poverty of the country, decay of manufactures, and prohibition of the chief exports doubtless partly accounted for this. Import trade was also affected by the enforcement of English regulations and restraints, especially by the Navigation Act of 1651, which forbade the import of

goods into any of the Commonwealth dominions except
in native ships, or in ships belonging to the country
whence the goods were brought[1]. The Scots had lost
a number of ships, and could not carry on their trade
without the help of foreigners. They begged for permission to transport their coal and salt to " whatsoever
places within or without this Island in what boddomes
the merchant may be best served with for their advantage[2]." They also desired to import goods from France
and Spain in foreign ships. Foreign salt was necessary
for the fish-curing, and they had some difficulty in securing a sufficient supply in their own ships. There were,
too, some prohibitions of import of goods which " wee
cannot subsist without." French wines were amongst
these goods, and they had long been a principal import
into Scotland, in exchange for Scots salmon, herring and
plaiding.

During the war, the Scots lost a number of ships,
especially in 1650 and 1651. In June 1650, the Scottish
Parliament wrote to Lord Fairfax and to Sir Arthur
Hazelrigge complaining of the seizure of Scots ships
by English vessels[3]. Two months later Admiral Deane
commissioned Captain Penn to seize all the Scottish ships
he should meet with, and to deliver them into the hands
of the collectors of prize goods[4]. After the Dunbar defeat,
orders were given that all the boats of the ports round
Edinburgh should be seized, "for serving the Inglisches
thair demandis[5]." A number of ships belonging to Dundee

---

[1] Scobell, *Acts*, Part II., p. 176.   [2] *Royal Burghs*, III., p. 394.
[3] *Acts, Scotland*, VI., Part II., p. 585.
[4] *H. M. C. R., Portland Papers*, II., p. 69.
[5] Nicoll, p. 34.

and the Fife ports were taken too, as the English army gradually established its hold over the south of Scotland[1]. These vessels do not seem to have been restored after the declaration of union, for after the Restoration many complaints were made as to the seizure of ships during the "late Usurpation." Privateers and other enemies had also reduced the number of Scots ships, so altogether there can have been but few left with which to prosecute trade. The Scots had never built many of their own ships, they generally got them from the Dutch. Now difficulties were put in the way of their buying ships, by a duty levied on all such purchases. The Burghs complained that "the commissioners for the customs excys doe exact the 20 peny of custome and the 20 peny of excys of all schippis bocht from straingeris and brocht home for the necessarie service of the natioun and increas of tread which exactionis doe much frustrat and hinder the restoring of the decayed and lost schipping of this cuntrie[2]." Together with English shipping, but probably more in comparison with its value, Scottish trade suffered from the disturbed and unsafe state of the seas at this time. The Channel, the Straits and in fact all the coasts were infested with numerous enemies, Royalist privateers, Dutch and Spanish men of war, and pirates. Some efforts were made to guard the Scottish coasts, but with little effect. In 1656 Lord Broghill wrote to Thurloe: "Indeed, sir, it is a sad thing that all Scotland should be without one man of warr to guard the cost, when our next neighbours are our open ennemies, and take our ships dayley, and within this ten dayse a rich vessell of Aberdeene,

---

[1] *Diary of Mr John Lamont of Newton* (Maitland Club), p. 35.
[2] *Royal Burghs*, iii., p. 435.

which has almost broake that toune, which began to trade. 'Tis not here as in England, wher a loss does at most ruin a person: heire it does the whole trade. We have often complayned of this. I beseech you, Sir get us som speedy redress[1]." An appeal for convoys was one of the demands of the Royal Burghs, which, with demands for the free export of wool, etc., permission to use foreign ships, the maintenance of the staple port at Campvere, the lightening of the burden of taxation, were reiterated to the Parliament in London almost every year until 1660. There was so little trade that many sailors were out of work. In 1656 "many skipperis and maryneris wer takin to sea to serve the Inglisches. Mony of thame without compulsioun wer content to tak on and serve, thair being lytill or no imployment for thame utherwayes in tred or merchandice, the seas being foull with pirattis and robberis[2]."

There were also special hindrances to particular branches of Scottish commerce. She had had more trade with Holland than with any other country, and the Commonwealth wars with that country damaged their connection there very much, and also hindered their correspondence with other countries. It was suggested that the staple port at Campvere should be given up[3], partly no doubt in pursuance of the Cromwellian policy of freedom from regulation. The suggestion was not, however, carried out. The English authorities were also jealous of the Scottish trade with Holland, their great rival. The Council of State wrote to the Lord General on the subject: "We are informed of the great inconveniences

---

[1] *Thurloe State Papers*, IV., p. 741.   [2] Nicoll, p. 174.
[3] *Scottish Staple at Veere*, p. 209.

and mischiefs upon this Commonwealth by the freedom of
Trade driven into Scotland by the Dutch...they get the
main trade into their own hands, and beat out the English
...their commodities may as well be furnished by the
people of this nation from hence...we judge it would be
advisable to forbid the importation of any goods into
Scotland by the Dutch[1]." The Council were struck by
the ingratitude of the Scots in allowing this trade; "their
malignancy is such, notwithstanding all the favours they
have received from you...that they will buy nothing of
the English if they can have it from the Dutch."

Some Scots merchants seem to have joined in the
trade from England to the Baltic. The English Eastland
merchants at Dantzig petitioned the Council of State in
1651 to "Debarr all Scots Malignants and Forraigners any
Trade from England to this place." "Divers of ye Scottish
Nation," they say, are "great Traders for London[2]."

The war with Spain also hindered trade. "The Spanish
warre has wracked many of our merchants." The privateers
from Dunkirk were especially dreaded, so much so that
the Scots chiefly traded with England during the war.
When they ventured further afield, it was "under the
covert and pretext of being Dutch, in whose ports they
enter theyr shippis, and sayle with Dutch passes and
marineris, or else bring home theyr goods in Dutch
bottomes which are made over by bill of sale, and soe
become the shipps of the nation when they arrive there,
but once unladen they depart, and are then Dutch
bottomes againe[3]." This close Scottish connection with

---

[1] S. P. Domestic, Interregnum, xcvi., 318 (1650).   [2] Ibid., xv., 95.
[3] Report by Thomas Tucker upon the Settlement of the Revenues of
Excise and Customs in Scotland (Bannatyne Club) pp. 44, 45.

the Dutch, and the evasion of the Navigation Act, must both have been most distasteful to the English authorities.

The complete union of England and Scotland at this time was of but short duration, and it is therefore difficult to justify or condemn the project. But the elements of failure, in circumstances rather than in the actual scheme, are so obvious that one can hardly imagine ultimate success attending the experiment. Scotland was a conquered country, she was poverty stricken and desolate, she was far behind England in economic development, her chief commercial connections were with the Protectorate's greatest rivals. The union was forced upon her by England, again her national enemy. It had to be maintained by a garrison and an army of occupation; and for their support Scotland was heavily taxed. English commercial regulations were disastrous to Scottish commerce, and she had neither wealth nor time enough to reconstruct and reconstitute her industrial system. From the English point of view Scotland was a great financial burden, and a source of danger to her commercial system by her connection with the Dutch, and her infringement of English commercial legislation. Therefore it is not surprising that after the Restoration separation was desired by both countries. Nor it is hardly to be wondered at that nearly fifty years should elapse before a union was finally established.

CHAPTER IV

THE latter part of the seventeenth century is of far more interest than the earlier half in the consideration of the commercial relations of England and Scotland, and also in the economic history of Scotland. The country developed a great deal in these years, especially considering her depressed state at the beginning of the period. Doubtless she learned something from England, during the years of union, as to the organisation of industry and trade. Her experience then may also have shewn her the importance of trade, and of the wealth which it brings, as factors in determining the position of nations in Europe. Scotland's economical development shewed both countries that the form of relationship between them was most unsatisfactory. The English Parliament had no control over Scottish trade, and in several different directions the Scots infringed the English commercial system. In defiance of the Navigation Acts they traded with the Plantations, and supplied them with their own and with Dutch manufactures. They continued, as far as possible, to trade with France and Holland when England was at war with these countries, and refused to prohibit the import of their products. Across the border these prohibited foreign goods could be imported into England, and English prohibited commodities could be exported. Scotland drove a profitable trade in the export of English wool. Finally England was shewn that it was possible for Scotland to give extensive powers to a trading company, which might have been a rival to the great English companies, and which very nearly embroiled England with her political allies. On the other hand the Scots found themselves treated as foreigners in England. They required markets for their manufactures, but high tariffs kept out their goods, and entire prohibition checked their trade with the Plantations; English wars hindered their principal foreign trades; English influence and enmity destroyed any chances of success which their great national trading venture might have had. Both nations found the state of affairs impossible. England found that for political as well as economic reasons a union with Scotland would be advisable, and the fifty years of separation, enmity and misunderstanding ended in the consummation of a complete and incorporating union.

a. INDUSTRY

The condition of Scotland at the Restoration was such as to make any change welcome. The heavy taxation and enforcement of the English commercial system, after the devastation caused by the wars, had kept the country in a state of great poverty. Many of the new industries introduced by James and Charles had died out, and the long established manufactures of the country, linen cloth, plaiding, etc., had considerably decayed. There was also

very little money in the country with which to start new
manufactures. Nevertheless the first care of the restored
Parliament was to make provision for the King's revenue.
An annuity of £40,000 sterling was granted to him for
life[1]. This was made up of £8000 from the customs, and
£32,000 from the excise on beer, ale, aqua vitae and other
"strong waters." New customs rates were imposed, more
or less on a protective system. The chief part of the
revenue was raised by duties on foreign manufactured
goods, cloths, serges, hats, stockings, etc. Certain imports
were free altogether, materials for fishing, shipbuilding,
soap manufacturing, wool, flax, dying materials, etc., also
sugar brought from the Plantations in Scottish ships.

Further legislation dealt with industry. Both England
and France were at this time engaged in building up
strictly protective systems, in order to develop and
encourage their industry and trade. Scotland, influenced
by their example, by the damage which their system
inflicted on her trade, and by the necessity of attracting
capital to the country, also set about creating a protective
system, developing the principles of the Act of 1644. The
first attempts to encourage industry, as embodied in the
Acts of 1661, did not meet with much success. Accordingly in 1681 further Acts were passed which completed
a very strict system of protection of native industry, by
prohibition of the import of foreign manufactured goods,
and of the export of raw materials. This time the policy
was more successful, the country having recovered somewhat from the effects of the Civil Wars. Companies
were founded, for which a certain amount of capital came

[1] *Acts, Scotland*, VII., p. 88.

from England. Between 1693 and 1695 especially a number of companies were floated, including the Darien Company. In the latter a good deal of the capital of the country was locked up, and a series of bad harvests followed. The manufacturers found the English and other foreign markets practically closed against most of their manufactures, and the attempt to provide a colonial market of their own had failed. The first few years of the eighteenth century were a time of depression and discontent, during which the manufacturing and trading interests alike began to realise that in order to secure the necessary markets they must become commercially one with England.

To superintend the general interests of trade and industry the Parliament of 1661 passed an Act establishing a Council of Trade[1]. This was to consist of five of each estate, and was entrusted with the duties of establishing companies, endowing them with privileges, making and enforcing regulations regarding trade and manufactures. The privileges which the companies were to receive were enumerated in the "Act for erecting of Manufactories[2]." Strangers brought in by natives to teach or to set up new industries were to enjoy all the privileges of natives. Materials for manufactures were to be imported, and the manufactured goods exported duty free for nineteen years. The stock employed was to be free of taxes, and the manufactories were to be free from the quartering of soldiers on them. Another Act dealt with the companies for making linen and woollen cloths, etc.[3] The preamble to this Act states that "many good

---

[1] *Acts, Scotland*, vii., p. 273.   [2] *Ibid.*, p. 261.
[3] *Ibid.*, p. 255.

Spirites haveing aimed at the publict good, have for
want of sufficient stocks councill and assistance been
crushed by such undertakings." Therefore it is thought
necessary " to create and erect companies and societies for
manufactories...as the first moderne societies and companies for making of lining cloth," etc. No linen or
woollen cloth was to be exported except by members of
these companies, and they alone were to be free of
customs and excise for nineteen years. The export of
linen yarn and of skins and hides was also forbidden.
The importation of "made work" which was also manufactured in the kingdom was forbidden[1]. By these Acts
a definite scheme of protection of native industry was
established. The new companies were assured, as far as
legislation could assure them, of a supply of raw material
by the prohibition of the export of linen yarn, wool, skins,
etc., and by the freedom from import duty of necessary
foreign materials. At the same time their home market was
guaranteed by the prohibition of the import of manufactures similar to their own. It must always be remembered, however, that this system was far more complete in
theory than in practice, and that the laws regulating
import and export were in fact but little observed.
There were now no complaints of the prohibition of the
export of wool and hides as there were under the
Protectorate Government, but this is far more likely to
be due to a lax observance of the law than to the supply
being entirely engrossed by the manufacturers.

By further legislation encouragement was given to
industry by the imposition in 1663 of heavy duties on
English cloth and other commodities[2], in retaliation for

Acts, Scotland, vii., p. 284.   [2] *Ibid.*, p. 465.

the English Navigation Acts. But the country was for
the first few years after the Restoration too poor to take
advantage of these encouragements. The English wars
with Holland, which began in 1664, were also a very
serious check to Scottish trade. Rothes, the Commissioner, wrote many letters to Lauderdale in 1665
and 1666, asserting the poverty of the country, and its
inability to raise either troops or money. "It is almost
impossible for this kingdom to raise money," he writes—
his spelling is corrected—"being so impoverished and
harassed with the late miserable troubles and rebellions
that our poverty is not to be expressed[1]." "As I hope to
be saved, this country is so exhausted that they are not
in a capacity to do anything as to money, but God help
us[2]." "We in this kingdom are wilful and proud and
necessitous even to beggary so consequently a ticklish
people to deal with."

Some progress was made, nevertheless, especially in
Glasgow, which had suffered less from the troubles than
the towns in the east. In 1667 soap-works were started
there, in which nine "persons of distinction" were interested, to the extent of £1500 sterling each. In the
same year and in 1669 sugar manufactories were founded,
the Easter and the Wester Sugar Works. In these nine
people were engaged, and taking advantage of the Act of
1661 each had a foreigner as "master boiler," a German
and a Dutchman[3]. Further information about these two
works is given in a petition of their master to Parliament
in 1681. In this he asserts that the price of manufactured

[1] *Lauderdale Papers* (Camden Society), I., p. 211.

[2] *Ibid.*, p. 215.

[3] *History of Glasgow*, J. McUre, p. 227.

sugar has been much reduced, and now is sold at only
8s. Scots. Also Scottish manufactures are exported to
Virginia and the Caribbee islands, whence the raw sugar
is brought. The only "Benefit and advantage" to the
manufacturers themselves, consisted in the export of
molasses, "which is the coursest part of the sugar," to
Holland and the eastern countries. But the Dutch
finding themselves injured by this trade have forbidden
the import of molasses, and heavy impositions have been
laid upon it by the eastern countries. The manufacturers
have therefore begun to manufacture strong waters instead of molasses and beg that these may be free of any
excise. This was granted, and all former privileges were
renewed[1]. A paper manufactory was also started in
1675[2]. The only other industry in which there is much
trace of progress being made during the early years of the
period was in fishing. The Act for establishing fishing
companies in 1661[3] had had no effect, and so in 1670
efforts were again made to encourage this industry. One
company was formed, with exclusive rights of fishing and
trade, and all the privileges of companies formed under
the Act of 1661. They were also granted the monopoly
of trading to Muscovy, Greenland, Iceland, and other
northern parts[4]. To this company Charles subscribed
£5000 and the total capital amounted to £25,000[5].
Proclamation was made at the same time forbidding
foreigners from fishing on the coasts. Unfortunately the
future career of this company was not very successful.

---

[1] S. P. C. R., 6 March 1679.
[2] Parliamentary Papers, xi., 32 (General Register House).
[3] Acts, Scotland, vii., p. 259.   [4] S. P. C. R., 26 June 1670.
[5] Memoirs of the affairs of Scotland, Sir George Mackenzie, p. 183.

According to the account of a merchant travelling in
Scotland in 1672 there had been but little advance made
in industry by that time. His account however seems to be
more prejudiced than dependable. His name was Dennis
de Repas, and he had travelled over most of Europe. He
wrote to Sir Edward Harley, vilifying Scotland and the
Scots. "I may assure your honour that in all my
travels...I never saw a nation in general more nasty, lazy,
and least ingenious in matter of manufactures than they
are....Except in great towns, they do not bake bread
though they may have plentiful of corn, but make
nastily a kind of stuff with oat half grinded which they
do call 'cake' which hath no more taste nor relish than
a piece of wooden trencher....I do speak so much of
Scotland, by reason that being your neighbours I do
wonder that they do not take something after the
English, which through all the world are counted the
most ingenious in all manner of manufactures[1]." The only
manufactures which he allows to them are those of plaiding
and of stockings, but the latter are "most nastily made."

The fact was that the country was too exhausted, by
the Civil and then by the Dutch wars, to really profit by
the legislation of 1661. No new manufactures were sent
abroad. Salmon, stockings, plaiding, linen, tallow, coals,
salt and skins were still the principal exports. Plaiding
and linen were however both manufactured and exported
in greater quantities. England was a great market for
linen. In 1672, 488,800 ells were carried thither overland
from Glasgow alone[2], while large quantities were entered

[1] *H. M. C. R., Portland Papers,* iii., p. 327.

[2] *Papers relating to Customs and Foreign Excise,* Vol. ii. (General
Register House).

at all the Border customs houses, and a great deal was also sent by sea.

After some years affairs began to improve, and in 1681 Parliament again turned their attention to industry. A complete system of protection was evolved, and this time there were manufacturers who were able to take advantage of it. During the next fifteen years, especially from 1690 to 1695, many manufactories were established, with varying success. One difficulty faced them all and gradually became more pressing—the difficulty of finding markets. The demand of the home market was small, France and England had closed their markets to some Scottish manufactures, and though trade with the Plantations was carried on, the fact that it was forbidden was naturally a hindrance to it. The merchants and manufacturers therefore gradually came to recognise the necessity of union with England, in order to provide markets for their goods.

The "Act for Encourageing Trade and Manufactories[1]" of 1681 ratified the Act of 1661, and also bestowed further privileges. The import of foreign materials made of wool, cotton, lint, gold or silver thread was prohibited, also of stockings, shoes, and some silks. The duties were removed from the import of goods to be used in the manufactories, and from the export of the manufactured articles, for nineteen years. All stock was freed from taxation, and the employés from military service for seven years. All works that had been set up or that were to be set up, were to be declared manufactories by Act of Parliament, in order that they might enjoy these privileges and immunities. Under this Act about fifty undertakings were erected into manufactories, and received these

[1] *Acts, Scotland*, viii., p. 348.

extensive privileges. Most of these were jointstock companies. Dr Scott gives an estimate of the capital employed in these works. The amount subscribed to some of them is recorded—the Royal Fishing Company £25,000, the Glasgow Soap Company £11,700, one of the Glasgow Sugar Works £10,000, the Scots Paper Manufactory £4000, the Bank of Scotland £10,000, the Glasgow Rope Company £3333, and the Linen Company about £10,000. Calculating from these figures, Dr Scott estimates the total capital employed at about £194,033[1]. Some of this was contributed by English undertakers, of whom a number were interested in Scottish undertakings. Foreign help was received too from some Huguenot refugees, skilled artisans, whose knowledge of the methods of cloth, silk, pottery, or other manufactures was of great value to the new companies. Foreign "tradesmen and merchants" were received as burgesses and freemen in the larger royal burghs on payment of £20 Scots, and in the smaller for £10 Scots[2].

As has been said, the regulations regarding import and export were never strictly enforced. Only two years after the Act of 1681, the Privy Council found it necessary again to forbid by Proclamation the importation of goods made of wool or lint[3]. Various petitions from cloth manufacturers shew that woollen cloth continued to be imported, partly, no doubt, because the manufacturers could not supply sufficient quantities of certain varieties, and because some Scots were unpatriotic enough to prefer

[1] *Records of a Scottish Cloth Manufactory at New Mills*, ed. by W. R. Scott (Scottish History Society), pp. xxxiv—xlvi.

[2] *Parliamentary Papers*, xv., 60.

[3] *S. P. C. R.*, 10 Aug. 1683.

the finer kinds of cloth which were not made in Scotland. Most of this imported cloth was English. In 1698 it was suggested that the import of woollen manufactures should be forbidden and penalised by a heavy imposition, or that the wearing of any wool not made in the kingdom should be prohibited, "which will be more civil but less effectuall[1]." Soon after this a number of people banded themselves together, and drew up a "Resolve containing a plain and direct Ingagement against the wearing of Forraign Cloths and making use of certain Forraign Liquors." This was presented both to "single persons and Societies for Concurrence." But any "Leagues or Bonds" were "reprobat by law," and, as the Resolve manifestly came under that category, all persons were forbidden to engage in it[2]. In 1701 the agitations of the manufacturers were successful, and the importation of both woollen and silk materials was again forbidden[3]. Frequent agitation was also made to enforce the acts dealing with the export of raw material, especially of wool. The foreign trade in wool was large, and of great advantage to the wool growers, who declared that the home demand for their wool was so small that they would be ruined were they not allowed to export. The manufacturers on the other hand declared that the reason that the cloth works did not flourish as they ought, was that they had difficulty in securing a sufficient supply of wool. The town of Aberdeen in 1693 declared that "since the exportatione therof" (i.e. of wool) "may tend to the utter ruine of woolling manufactories in this kingdome which in former tymes brought in considerable

---

[1] *Parliamentary Papers*, xv., 86[2].
[2] Proclamation, 1700, General Register House.
[3] *Acts, Scotland*, x., pp. 275, 280.

coyned money to the Countrie, but by the late considerable Exportatione of the said Commoditie vertuous people
are forced either to give over the making of woolling
manufactorie or to make it so slight as renders it unvend-
able abroad[1]." Aberdeenshire was one of the chief seats
of the manufacture. These and other like arguments
were successful, and in 1701 the export of wool was
forbidden[2]. It was still smuggled out of the country to
some extent, but on the whole the Act was said to be of
great advantage.

The trade in the old established cloth manufacture
had decayed very much. In 1674 about 400,000 ells of
plaiding had been exported from Aberdeenshire, at 11s. 6d.
per ell. In 1694 and until 1700 the trade had declined,
and only about 80,000 ells yearly at 6s. or 7s. per ell were
sent away. After the Act of 1701 the trade recovered
again, and about 200,000 ells, at the old price, were
exported in 1701 and 1702[3]. The triumph of the manufacture was short-lived, however, for in 1704 the export of
wool was again allowed[4].

That the Acts regarding import and export were
observed to some extent is shewn by the grants of abatements made to the farmers of the customs, after Acts
prohibiting some imports or exports were passed. In 1681
the tacksmen declared that "the restraint...being so
Comprehensive and relateing to a great part of the
subject of trade hes made a present Interruption of all
trade the merchands being at a stand and not knowing

---

[1] *Parliamentary Papers*, xiv., 101.

[2] *Acts, Scotland*, x., p. 277.

[3] *Parliamentary Papers*, xiv., 65.

[4] *Acts, Scotland*, xi., p. 190.

what to Import[1]." When the export of linen yarn
was forbidden in 1693, they received an abatement of
£591. 3s. 8d. This was calculated from the amount of
linen yarn exported in 1692—101,272 pounds, on which
the duty was £591. 17s. 0d.[2] Later the tacksmen of the
customs between 1697 and 1702 claimed an abatement of
£14,159. 11s. 4d., in consideration of their losses by the
various Acts of 1698, 1699 and 1701, prohibiting the
export of wool and the import of foreign woollen manufactures[3].

Having now touched upon the disadvantages of the
system it is necessary to glance at the degree of success
which attended it. As has been said, about fifty new
manufactories were started. Of these the woollen and
linen were the most important. Seven works for manufacturing woollen cloths of different kinds were erected
between 1681 and 1695, and two in 1703. They chiefly
manufactured the coarser sorts of materials, serges, baizes,
etc., and it was in this line that they were most successful,
as there were not so many rivals with whom to compete.
Coarse cloth had a good sale in the Plantations, it was
cheap and strong and useful for servants' wear. According
to the writer of *A Representation of the Advantages...
of Manufactories* (1683)[4], a great deal was sent to
Holland and some was even smuggled into England.
The finer serges found good markets in Holland, Hamburg
and Spain. The minutes of the New Mills Manufactory
afford a good deal of information as to the working of the

---

[1] *Customs, Miscellaneous Papers*, 1592–1690.
[2] *Customs and Foreign Excise*, Vol. VII.
[3] *Customs, Miscellaneous Papers*, 1692–1707.
[4] Advocates' Library, Pamphlets, Vol. LXXXVII.

cloth works. Four varieties of cloth were made, the finest with Spanish wool only, the next quality with Spanish and English wools mixed, the third with English, and the coarsest with Scottish wool alone[1]. This company never seemed to have large quantities in stock, nor to be able to provide a supply quickly. The directors were occasionally applied to to supply cloth suitable for uniforms, "to distinguish sojers from other sculking and vagrant persons," but generally failed to have enough material by the required time, and licences had usually to be given to import the necessary amount from England. The manufacture on the whole, however, had advanced a great deal since the beginning of the century, and the improvement was nearly all subsequent to the passing of the protective legislation. That its prosperity was due to protection, and that without protection it could not stand, was obvious after the union, when the Scottish cloth manufacture suffered very much from the free competition of the English manufactures.

The linen manufacture was more successful. For one thing the country was more adapted for it, and also it was easier to find a market for linen than for cloth. A special Act dealing with this manufacture was passed in 1693, forbidding the export of linen yarn, and providing for the import of linen yarn and export of cloth duty free[2]. It was thought that it would be a particularly suitable time for setting up a linen manufactory, "when the seas are troublesome and tradesmen abroad ruined with warrs," as it might be possible to get the trade of supplying England with those cloths which the French and Dutch now sent

[1] *New Mills Minutes*, p. 55.   [2] *Acts, Scotland*, IX., p. 311.

her[1]. One manufactory was founded in this year at Leith, which exported in the year 1693–4, £2012. 3s. 5d. value of linen. The custom remitted on this was £427. 4s., and on the goods imported for its use £308. 19s.[2] Further encouragement was given by an Act making burial in Scots linen compulsory[3]. A good deal of linen was exported to the Plantations, and also to Holland, Spain and England. It was in fact the most important of all Scottish imports to England, amounting to about £40,000 value yearly. On the whole the linen industry was perhaps the most important of all the industries, at any rate from the point of view of the export trade. Those engaged in it were anxious for the union, as they expected to profit greatly by the increased opportunities for export to the Plantations.

The manufacture of sugar was also a flourishing one. New works were founded at Leith, Glasgow[4], and elsewhere. In connection with one of these works a distillery was established, to make spirits out of molasses. This, it was said, would be of great advantage to trade. Not only would more sugar be imported from the Plantations, and more woollens and other manufactures sent there, but spirits would be made at home instead of being imported from England. The Fishing Company established in 1670 was not so successful however. Another Act was passed in 1685 giving many privileges to those engaged in the fishing trade[5], but no great advantage was taken of it. Most of the pamphlets which advocate the union deplore

---

[1] *Parliamentary Papers*, XIX., 100.

[2] *Customs and Foreign Excise*, Vol. VII.

[3] *Acts, Scotland*, IX., p. 461.

[4] *Ibid.*, p. 491; x., p. 66.   [5] *Ibid.*, IX., p. 202.

the neglect of this trade, and the loss of the wealth which it should bring to the country, most of which, they assert, goes to the Dutch. Other works were erected for the manufacture of soap, silk, glass, salt, starch, ropes, paper, oil, gunpowder, etc. Of great importance was the founding of the Bank of Scotland in 1695[1], the " first instance of a private joint stock bank formed by private persons for the express purpose of making a trade of banking, wholly unconnected with the State, and dependent on their own private capital[2]." It was not, however, till after the union that the Bank proved its true usefulness to the country in the facilities which it gave for raising money to promote industry and agriculture. It was not until after the union also that any advance was made in agriculture, the practice of which continued very backward and on much the same lines throughout the seventeenth century.

As has been said, the promotion of industry received a check after the year 1695, due to the large investment of capital in the African Company, and to the bad harvests of the succeeding years. The harvest of 1695 was very bad, that of 1696 was worse, and 1697 was also a bad year. Complaints from all over the kingdom attest the widespread nature of the dearth. In Aberdeen " ther is on of the greatest skaircities of Victuall that ever you heard of." The famine in Inverness " is more calamitous then was ever felt heretofor in our age," while round Edinburgh many had not even been able to sow their land in 1696 because of the want of seed[3]. The dearth increased the

---

[1] *Acts, Scotland*, IX., p. 494.

[2] Macleod, *Theory and Practice of Banking*, I., p. 307.

[3] Papers relating to the Condition of the Excise, *Miscellaneous Papers*, 1692–1707.

discontent of the country.   After 1700 harvests improved again, but the want of markets was an ever present grievance.   The Lord Chancellor in his speech to Parliament in 1703 asserted that " Our Manufactures are very much improved but we have almost no forraign trade[1]." For this condition of affairs the union with England was blamed, but it was also commonly realised that it was the nature of the union that was at fault, and that the only means of remedy lay in a complete and incorporating union[2].

b. Trade with England

As has been said with the Restoration the union of England and Scotland came to an end, a result popular in both countries.   The Scots supposed that their position would be the same as during the reigns of James I and Charles I, that is, that they would be regarded as natives as far as shipping and foreign trade were concerned. The first year's legislation of the English Parliament soon. proved to them that they were mistaken.   The Navigation Act of 1660[3] shewed that only the people of " England or Ireland Dominion of Wales or Towne of Berwick upon Tweede" were to be allowed to share in English trade, plantation, foreign or coasting.   Impositions and restrictions on the passage of goods between England and Scotland proved that Scotland was now looked upon as a foreign country.   The attitude of England was described

[1] *Acts, Scotland*, xi., Appendix, p. 9.

[2] For Scottish industry in this period see articles by W. R. Scott on Scottish Industrial Undertakings before the Union.   *Scottish Historical Review*, 1903–4.

[3] 12 Car. II, c. 18.

in the preamble of one of the Acts of 1660 : "And to the
intent that the full and best Use and benefit of the
principall native Commodities of the same Kingdomes
and Dominion" (i.e. of England, Ireland and Wales), "may
come redound and be unto and amongst the Subjects and
Inhabitants of the same and not unto or amongst the
Subjects and Inhabitants of the Realme of Scotland, or of
any Forraigne Realmes or States[1]." Scotland had been a
financial burden to England when they were under the
rule of the same Parliament, and for this and other reasons
the parliamentary union was discontinued. At this time
England was developing a strongly protective system, both
industrial and commercial. Before the Civil Wars the
regulations had not been so severe, nor so strictly enforced,
and had been organised and administered by the King
and his Council. But after the Restoration Parliament
regulated the economic life of the country. They considered that the commercial incorporation of Scotland
could be of no benefit to England, and, as they could
not regulate or supervise Scottish trade in any way,
it might be harmful. The Scots import and export
restrictions differed from the English, and therefore prohibited commodities might be imported to or exported
from England through Scotland. The Scots had had no
share in settling the Plantations, and yet they might set
up a trade with them, and deprive England of some of
the advantage which should accrue to her alone. Also the
Scots had much trade and connection with Holland, and
the English feared that the Dutch might, under cover of
the Scots, obtain some share in English Plantation trade,

[1] 12 Car. II, c. 32.

and that Scotland might become a centre whence the
Dutch should supply the Continent with English Plantation commodities. Therefore Scotland was to be allowed
no share in English commerce, and was in fact treated
like a foreign country. In both countries, but especially
in Scotland, the old mutual dislike was still in existence,
only increased by the late union. Mackenzie declares that
" Scotland was entirely freed from the English soldiers and
garrisons; and Lauderdale upon that accompt deserved
well of his country and magnified himself in it as a great
testimony of his love for Scotland...."

One of the first acts of the English Parliament of 1660
was to draw up new " Rates of Merchandise," in which
duties were imposed on various Scots commodities, coals,
beef, linen, skins, yarn, etc.[1] Later, a tax of $\frac{1}{2}d.$ per
gallon was put on Scots salt[2]. Also a tax of 20s. per head
was imposed on cattle brought into England from Scotland
between August 20 and December 20[3]; and of 10s. per
tun on Scots beer[4]. All goods brought from Scotland
into England had to be entered at Berwick or Carlisle[5].
Then too the exportation of certain goods from England
into Scotland was prohibited, especially wool[6] and hides[7].
Successive Acts dealt with navigation, excluding the Scots
from trade with the Plantations and from any share in
English coasting or foreign trade[8]. These Acts raised a
great outcry in Scotland, especially from the Convention of
Royal Burghs. After petitions for relief from the various

[1] 12 Car. II, c. 4.   [2] 14 Car. II, c. 11.
[3] 15 Car. II, c. 7.   [4] 18 and 19 Car. II, c. 5.
[5] 14 Car. II, c. 11.   [6] 12 Car. II, c. 32.
[7] 14 Car. II, c. 7.
   12 Car. II, c. 18; 14 Car. II, c. 11; 15 Car. II, c. 7.

impositions had been sent in without effect, the Scots proceeded to retaliation. In 1661 their Parliament passed an Act of Navigation on very much the same lines as the English Act, but only to be put into force against English or Irish ships as long as Scottish ships were excluded from English and Irish trade[1]. Of greater importance was the "Act for ane new Imposition on English Commodities[2]." The preamble declared that "the endeavours of such persons as are setting up manufactories and trades have been and are much retarded by the importation of such forraign commodities as may be made within the Kingdome." Heavy impositions were therefore laid on English cloths, hats, gloves, etc., and a duty of 80˙ per cent. on all goods not particularly specified in the Act. Before this Act was passed it had been found that the English imports to Scotland were twenty times greater than the Scots to England[3]. The Act was at the time intended rather for retaliation than for protection, for the Privy Council was given power to remove all the impositions, as soon as "trade and commerce shall be restored to the condition it was in dureing the reigne of his Maiestie's father and Grandfather of blessed memory." The Act had some of the desired effect, in that the merchants and others trading to Scotland felt the impositions severely, and also petitioned the King to restore trade to the same condition as in the earlier part of the century. Great quantities of English manufactures and of English Plantation commodities had been imported to Scotland, and now, they said, "thousands of families who gett a comfortable sub-

---

[1] *Acts, Scotland*, VII., p. 257.

[2] *Ibid.*, p. 465.

[3] *S. P. Domestic, Charles II*, LXXVI., 11.

sistence in ye management of that Trade are now exposed to want and beggary[1]."

The whole question of the regulations of trade between the two countries was brought before the House of Commons and the Council of Trade. They came to the conclusion that, as the imports from England to Scotland were considerable, the restraints on Scottish imports should be removed, to induce the Scots to take off their new duties on English goods. With regard to shipping they advocated the admission of the Scots to all trade, with this exception, they "shall not have intercourse or Trade from Scotland with any English Plantations[2]." Notwithstanding the Council's opinion, however, the restraints were not removed. The Scots felt the restrictions very heavily. In 1665 the Scottish Privy Council wrote to Charles: "There hes bein so many addresses made to us for representing the sufferings of this Kingdome by the want of trade occasioned by the late act of your Parliament of England imposing so great customes upon our native commodities that our whole trade with that Kingdome is totally destroyed....That wee found it our deuty humbly to intreat your Ma^{ty} to interpose your authority for taking off these acts and restraints in behalf of this Kingdome and for that effect to make use of the late act of your Maties Parliament here Remitting wholly to your Ma^{ty} the taking off of any imposition or restraint imposed in order to English commodities[3]." Inspired by Charles, in 1667 commissioners from both kingdoms were appointed, and authorised to treat concerning freedom of trade. The Scottish commissioners demanded the repeal

---

[1] S. P. Col., East India Entry Book, i., p. 79.
[2] Ibid., p. 83.   [3] S. P. C. R., 5 May 1665.

of the Navigation Acts, as far as Scotland was concerned ;
the removal of the impositions on linen, cattle, salt, beer ;
of the unusual customs imposed of late in Northumberland and Cumberland ; and also of the prohibition of the
export of English wool and hides into Scotland[1]. The
English commissioners demanded that all impositions on
English goods in Scotland should be removed, and proposed some concessions to the Scottish demands[2]. On the
question of the Navigation Acts the commissioners came
to a deadlock. The Scots insisted that this point should
be settled first[3]. The English offered some minor concessions, liberty to import timber from the Baltic, and
goods from Turkey and Muscovy for six years, but refused
to allow any share in the Plantation trade. This was the
liberty which the Scots particularly desired, and so the
negotiations came to an end without any treaty being
made. The English commissioners gave their reasons in
answer to the Scottish argument that they should be
allowed the same freedom as Ireland. "And whereas
your Lopps doe in severall places give hints at Ireland,
and seeme to make it a ground why this and other
Priviledges should be granted to Scotland, because granted
to Ireland the answere is most cleare and obvious (vizt.)
that Ireland is not onely under one King with Us, as
Scotland but belongs unto and is an Appendix of the
Crowne of England, and Lawes made in the Parliament of
England doe binde them, and no Law can be enacted by
the Parliament of Ireland but what passeth of Privy
Councell of England...by all which it is absolutely in our
power when we grant priviledges to them to compell and

[1] S. P. Domestic, Charles II, ccxxxiv., 28.
[2] Ibid., ccxlv., 185.   [3] Ibid., ccxxxiii., 60.

keep them up to the restrictions and limitacions of them, all which is quite otherwise in relacon to Scotland[1]." The English traders regretted the failure of the negotiations. They had had a flourishing trade with Scotland, but had " for some late years beene much Interrupted in their said Trades to the endangering their creditts and Estates, by reason of severall penall laws made in England and Scotland for Imposing divers high Dutyes and forfeitures on the Manufactures and Commodities of each Nation[2]."

The Lord Keeper, in his speech to Parliament in October 1669, declared that the negotiations had " produced no effect, unless it were a Conviction of the Difficulty if not impossibility of settling it in any other way than by a nearer and more complete Union of the two Kingdoms." Accordingly, to meet the King's wishes, commissioners were appointed to treat for a complete union, but their negotiations were also unsuccessful. Neither country in fact was yet ready for a union. The Scots, even though they were extremely anxious for freedom of trade with the Plantations, did not wish to pay the price of an entire union for it. According to Mackenzie, " The people upon the first news of the Union shew a great aversion for it, and its contrivers...nor would the proposal of an Union have been less acceptable to the people at any time than at this, in which the remembrance of their oppression from the Usurper was yet fresh with them[3]." Lauderdale was even more emphatic, " Yow cannot imagine what aversion is generally in this kingdom to

---

[1] *S. P. Domestic, Charles II*, ccxxxvi., 133.

[2] *Ibid.*, ccxli., 88. i.

[3] *Mackenzie's Memoirs*, pp. 138—139.

the Union. The indeavour to have made us slaves by garrisons and the ruine of our trade by severe lawes in England frights all ranks of men from having to doe with England[1]." Scots pride was against any proposal for union coming from their side. They did not wish to "seem so very fond and hastie before it appeared whither England wold hearken to this motion or not." England, on the whole, was indifferent to the question. Her statesmen, although they recognised that they had no control over the Scots Parliament, did not seem to imagine that Scotland could ever be in a position to menace English prosperity and power. Nor did they realise that England would not be able to export as many commodities to Scotland as before, and that the Scots would have to supply themselves by importing more manufactures from abroad, probably from Holland, or by setting up more manufactures of their own.

Until the end of William's reign no more negotiations for freedom of trade were opened. James VII on his accession assured the Scottish Parliament that he would "endeavour with all imaginable Care to open a free intercourse of Trade with His Kingdom of England," but nothing came of his declaration. After the Revolution the Scots reproached themselves for not having secured trade privileges from England, before they voted the crown to William and Mary. No concessions were made to them either then or later in William's reign.

In spite of the restrictions trade between Scotland and England did not come to a total standstill. The chief Scottish commodities imported into England were cattle, salt and linen, and from the early years of James's reign

[1] *Lauderdale Papers*, II., p. 154.

until the Restoration no special impositions had been laid
upon these articles in England. Coal, fish and skins were
also imported.

For two or three years after 1660 cattle were not
included in the list of Scots commodities on which new
duties were imposed. Tolls had to be paid as before however on cattle entering Cumberland, Westmoreland, and
Carlisle. In 1662, 318,574 cattle from Scotland passed
through Carlisle, paying eightpence per head as toll there[1].
In the same year Sharp wrote to Lauderdale, telling him
that there was a rumour current in Scotland that the
English Parliament intended to prohibit the importation
of Scots cattle. "The money arysing by this trade," he
says, " hes been the most sure and considerable stock for
the returns of money" from England[2]. The report was
partly true, for in 1663 the Act for the Encouragement of
Trade imposed a duty of 20s. on all Scots cattle imported
between August 20 and December 20[3]. The Burghs
complained that the " great and heavie impositionis laitlie
laid be the parliament of England upon coall salt bestiall
and wther native comodities of this Kingdome is in effect
equivalent to ane direct prohibitione of the importing of
any such comodities from Scotland to England[4]." The
trade nevertheless seems to have continued, though doubtless somewhat diminished. In 1665 the Grand Juries of
Yorkshire, in a petition to the House of Commons, complained of the importation of Scottish and Irish cattle.
It was the occasion of " the greate want of money and
decay of trade in this Country." The cattle " being fedd

[1] S. P. Domestic, Charles II, lxxviii., 11.
[2] Lauderdale Papers, i., p. 131.   [3] 15 Car. II, c. 7.
[4] Royal Burghs, iii., p. 563.

maintained and fatted with farre lesse charge, then can possibly be done in England, they fill and quitt the Marketts…and undersell those of English breed and feeding soe much that the ffarmers who formerly furnished other parts must and doe give over breeding and are forced to buy for themselves of that sort to their utter undoing and the Grasier cannot sell his fatt Cattle for the price they cost whereby industry is layed aside trade decayed and putt into the hand of Strangers, our coyne carried out of the Kingdome, by those who buy little if anything amongst us[1]." The imposition was objected to by the commissioners who treated for freedom of trade, and, though not apparently in connection with the negotiations, an Act of the English Council declared that "no duetie ought to be demanded or receaved for any Scots cattle coming into England[2]." After this the trade continued without any interruption, about 15,000 of the best Scottish black cattle being sent to England every year. In 1704 the importation was forbidden by the Act for securing England from Dangers from Scotland[3]. Although this Act was soon repealed no cattle were sent into England until the treaty of Union had been concluded. The Scots cattle dealers were more fortunate than the Irish. For, by the Act of 1663, whereas the Scots cattle paid a duty on entering England between August and December, the Irish cattle were liable between July 1 and December. This duty was said almost to destroy the Irish cattle trade[4], but a further blow was dealt it when in 1666 Irish cattle were prohibited from being imported

[1] *S. P. Domestic, Charles II*, cxxxiii., 90.
[2] *S. P. C. R.*, 6 May 1669.   [3] 3 & 4 A., c. 7.
[4] Carte, *Life of James, 1st Duke of Ormonde*, ii., p. 317.

into England at all[1]. In spite of some agitation Scots
cattle were not included in this prohibition.

Scots linen was another important import into England.
This also had been free of duty until the Restoration,
when a duty of £3 was imposed on every hundred ells
of Scottish "Twill or Ticking[2]." Although complaints
were made of this, as of all the impositions on Scottish
imports, the trade in linen does not seem to have been
very much affected by the duty. It remained the same
until 1690, but some years before that there was some
interruption in the trade. The "Noblemen and Gentlemen of Scotland and their tenents who make Lining
cloath" sent in a petition to the Council in 1684. In this
they declared that the manufacture of linen was one of
the principal industries of Scotland, and that it was
chiefly exported to England. "Bot of late this trade hes
bein stopt and the petitioners countrymen whipt like
malefactors through severall towns for following of their
trade and very many of them have been forced to give
bond never to return by which besides the affront and
ignominy these prejudices aryse to the nation." The ten
or twelve thousand men employed formerly in the trade
"are now rendered miserable and ane burden both to
themselves and the Government," while the loss to his
Majesty's customs is great[3]. This interruption can only
have been temporary, for new works for making linen
cloth were set up between 1690 and 1695. One of these
was largely financed and worked by Englishmen[4]. The
duty on Scots linen in England was raised in 1690 from

[1] 18 Car. II, c. 23.   [2] 12 Car. II, c. 4.
[3] *S. P. C. R.*, 2 Dec. 1684.
[4] *Royal Burghs*, iv., p. 194.

£6. 17s. 9d. per hundred pounds value to £10. 8s. 0¾d.[1],
and again in 1698 to £15. 3s. 0¾d.[2]   The increases in
the duty decreased the sale somewhat, and the linen
unsold in England became a drug on the market.
The Scots already sent enough to continental markets
to supply the demand there, and as much as possible
to the Plantations.   English anxiety to keep the Scots
out of the colonial market was evident in an Act passed
in 1704, "to permit the exportation of Irish cloth to
the Plantations and to prohibit the Importation of
Scotch linen into Ireland[3]."   This was passed just after
the Act for securing England from the dangers from Acts
passed in Scotland, and was doubtless inspired by the
same feeling.   The authorities found that the close connection of Scotland with the north of Ireland would lead
to Scots linen being sent, under cover of Irish linen, to
the Plantations.   In spite of the high duties on linen it
was one of the most important Scottish imports into
England, generally amounting to about £40,000 value, or
more, in the year.   This was generally more than half the
whole total value of Scottish imports into England.

The trade in salt had been, ever since the Union of
1603, a fruitful source of discord between the two
countries.   To this the latter half of the century was no
exception.   One of the first cares of the Convention of
Burghs was to petition that no duty should be laid upon
coal and salt, "that tread which is of greatest concernment
of any commoditie cumes fra this kingdome[4]."   The Privy
Council also sent in a petition to the same effect, but in

---

[1] British Museum, Additional MSS. 280791.
[2] 9 Gul. III, c. 45.   [3] 3 & 4 A, c. 7.
[4] *Royal Burghs*, III., p. 511.

1662 a duty of eightpence per wey (a halfpenny per gallon) was imposed on Scots salt coming into England[1]. This was "in effect a restraint upon that commodity they not being able to sell at such a rate." As it was "a mater that concerns the whole Kingdome and of great importance[2]," the Privy Council were desired to lay the matter before Charles, but the duty was not removed. During the negotiations for a commercial treaty in 1668–9 many papers and petitions dealing with this subject were laid before the commissioners. The Scots wanted the duty to be reduced to a farthing per gallon, or to be abolished altogether, and they were supported by the traders in salt in the south of England. The manufacturers in and near North and South Shields and the north demanded that it should be continued at a halfpenny, and gave copious reasons in support of their petitions. The salt-works at Shields had, they said, become considerable about seventy years before, and had been much encouraged by the limitation of the yearly import of Scots salt in 1637. But the Scots "at there inrode upon England in 1644 violently destroyed of these salt workes at Sheilds and Sunderland to the number of 50 or 60 and thereby they made an open way for the Scotts trade of Salt with England and much impeded and prevented the Salt Trade for Sheilds undersellinge the Marketts in England. Whereupon the Parliament imposed in the year 1649 one penny halfepenny per Gallon on Scotch salt imported." But "the said duty being taken of upon the pretended union between England and Scotland Anº 1654 many of their salt works were thereby ruined and pulled in peices

---

[1] 14 Car. II, c. 11.   [2] *S. P. C. R.*, 23 Dec. 1662.

by the owners and most of the owners of the remaining
haste contracted great debts hitherto not discharged.
For the prevencon of the growth of that Evill and the
encouragement and preservacon of the said Manufacture
his Matie was gratiously pleased An° 1662 by and with
the desire of his Parliament, to lay the duty of ½d. per
Gallon upon all Scotts Salt imported into the Kingdom of
England as a Ballance of ye Manufacture in both Kingdomes[1]." The English manufacturers asserted that the
cost of making salt in Scotland was less than in England.
It could be made for £1. 4s. per wey in Scotland, but the
expenses in England were £1. 15s. 10d. Therefore the
duty was necessary in order to equalise matters. Cheaper
production in Scotland was accounted for by the low price
of coal, the low rate of wages, cheapness of food, and
cheapness of freight[2]. The Scots declared that if the duty
were maintained they would not be able to sell their salt
at all. Their supporters, English traders in Scots salt,
accused the Shields manufacturers of trying "to rayse the
Price of that Commodity upon your Majesties English
Subjects to what rate they think fitt." The Scots salt
was said to be of better quality and more fit for supplying
the Navy and the fishing trade. Since the duty was
levied they had not been able to buy or bring in Scots
salt, "notwithstanding any allegacons of the English Salt
makers for the cheaper making the said Commodity in
Scotland then in England." They were therefore forced
to use the Shields salt which was "so new and ill made
that a great part thereof wastes into Brine in the Ships[3]."
Nor were they able to get sufficient quantities of that,

---

[1] *S. P. Domestic, Charles II,* ccxxxiv., 197.
[2] *Ibid.,* 198.   [3] *Ibid.,* ccxlvi., 78.

and the price had already been raised from thirty-two to
forty shillings[1]. Charles himself was anxious to have the
duty reduced, and ordered that only a farthing should be
taken while the negotiations were going on. The commissioners protested against his making any move in the
matter. They were "sure that Your Majesty and the
board will not doe anything, wherby a just discourage-
ment shalbe put upon the English traders to the ruine of
many thousand familyes[2]." The ruin of Scottish families
and traders was evidently considered a matter of no
importance. The end of these lengthy deliberations was
that the duty of a halfpenny was continued. As a result
the import of Scots salt into England declined very much,
and by the end of the century only a very inconsiderable
amount was sent there.

The development of the Scottish protective system
brought with it heavy duties and prohibitions on the import of many manufactured commodities. From these
the English traders suffered considerably. It has already
been pointed out that the protective regulations were not
strictly enforced, but nevertheless English imports to
Scotland decreased. For some years previous to 1668 it
was said that the English imports to Scotland did "over-
ballance what went out of Scotland to England fyftie or
threescore thousand pounds stirling per annum." But
during the ten or twelve years previous to the Union, the
average value of imports into Scotland was not much more
than £65,000 yearly, while the value of Scottish imports
into England was about £10,000 more. The English
import was made up of small quantities of a number of
commodities, of which hops, tanned leather, silk, both

[1] *S. P. Domestic, Charles II*, ccxlvii., 12. i.   [2] *Ibid.*, ccxlvi., 129.

"thrown" and "wrought," tobacco, sugar, and dyeing materials were the most important[1]. The "woollens" imported were not a large quantity after the "Act discharging the importing and wearing of Forreign Woollen Manufacture[2]" of 1701 was passed. After that between £2000 and £3000 worth only was imported, or was entered in the customs books yearly. There was doubtless a great deal of smuggling between the two countries, especially in wool, of which the export from England now, as during the earlier period, was strictly prohibited. Charles's first Parliament hastened to pass "An Act for prohibiting the Exportation of Wooll, Woollfells Fullers Earth or any kind of Scouring Earth" from England into the "Kingdome of Scotland or any forreigne parts[3]." Irish wool was only allowed to be sent to England. Two years later because "great numbers of Sheep and great quantities of Wooll… are secretly exported…into the Kingdome of Scotland and other Forraigne parts" the export was again prohibited[4]. Further complaints as to the export of wool to Scotland do not occur until the later years of the century. The gradually increasing Scottish cloth-works found English wool necessary for their manufactures. Several references are made in the minutes of the New Mills cloth company to their practice of getting wool from England. "The Master and George Home having made report of their journey into the south of Scotland and north of Ingland that they have settled with James Robson for buying of

---

[1] For the nature and amount of trade between Scotland and England 1697–1707, see Customs Accounts, Inspector-General's Ledger of Imports and Exports 1697–1707. (Public Record Office.)

[2] *Acts, Scotland*, x., p. 275.

[3] 12 Car. II, c. 32.   [4] 14 Car. II, c. 18.

wooll." On 19 July 1682, a certain George Archer, also engaged in buying wool, was to be told "to take notice especially of the risk on the Inglish side which the company will not bear the hazard of." Later the company decided to buy their English wool at the market in Edinburgh "as cheapest in probability." If the Edinburgh market had a regular supply of English wool there must have been a considerable trade in that commodity. But the Scots merchants found that it was still more profitable to export English wool to the Continent.

France, under Colbert's administration, had entered upon a policy of developing her trade and industry. England was extremely jealous of French power and influence, and the cloth manufacturers in particular feared French rivalry. The French makers of cloth were very anxious to obtain English wool to mix with their own, and offered very good prices for it. In Scotland the prospect of getting high prices abroad greatly encouraged the trade of bringing English wool across the Border. It was then exported to France or Holland, instead of being made up at home. This trade gradually increased, and a few years after the Revolution it had become a constant source of grievance to English authorities. In 1696 "An Act for the more effectual preventing the Exportation of Wooll" declared that "the several Inhabitants of the several Counties and Shires of this Realm next adjoining to the Kingdom of Scotland and to the Sea-Coasts do reap great Profit and Advantage by the Carrying out of Wooll, Wooll-fells...into the said Kingdom of Scotland, and exporting of them into France and other parts beyond the Seas....That from the first day of May 1696 no Wooll...shall be laid or loaden on any

Horse or other carriage whatsoever or shall be carried or
conveyed by Land to or from any Place or Places within
the said Counties next adjoining to the said Kingdom of
Scotland or within five miles of the Sea-coast...but
between Sun-rising and Sun-setting[1]." In 1698 "the
said Exportation is still notoriously continued," and fresh
regulations were therefore made[2]. Owners of wool within
ten miles of the coast in Kent or Sussex, or fifteen miles
of the Scottish borders, were ordered to give account to
the nearest officer of the amount of wool they had, and
where it was housed. They were also to give notice
before they removed any wool, and to say where it was to
be carried. Next year another statute dealt with the
export of wool from Ireland[3]. It was to be brought to
England only, and twelve ships and sloops were "con-
stantly to cruize on the coasts of England and Ireland
particularly betwixt the North of Ireland and Scotland,"
to seize all vessels suspected of carrying wool to Scotland
or to foreign ports.

The complaints made by the Board of Trade, the
manufacturers and others fully bear out the evidence of
these statutes. In November 1697, the Commissioners
for Trade and Plantations in a "Representation relating
to ye Gen[l] State of ye Trade of this Kingdom," declared
that the woollen manufactures were "much prejudiced
by the growth of the like Manufactures made in other
Countrys, much promoted by Wooll carryed from England,
Scotland and Ireland. Wee are Informed that great
Quantitys are frequently Landed in Holland from Scotland which wee Suppose is most carried thither out of

---

[1] 7 & 8 Gul. III, c. 28.   [2] 10 & 11 Gul. III, c. 40.
[3] 11 & 12 Gul. III, c. 10.

England or Ireland, particularly there was landed at
Rotterdam from Scotland in the beginning of October
last 982 Bags[1]." The Scots also sent English wool to
Sweden. "The King of Sweden did about the Year 1680
levy a duty of above 50 per cent. upon our Woollen Goods
imported thence, and encouraged Woollen Manufactures
in his own Dominions, Carried on by the help of Wooll
from England (as wee are informed) but Exported thither
by way of Scotland." In 1699 the Commissioners of the
Customs made special efforts to seize some of the vessels
concerned in this trade. "Being informed that notwithstanding all Endeavours to ye Contrary greate Quantitys
of Wooll were Carryed over ye Borders out of England
into Scotland and from thence shipt to Holland, France,
and other Partes of Europe. And being particularly
Advertised thereof from Leith in Scotland about ye latter
end of October last and that such Ships did often touch
in Yarmouth Road, They directed ye Collector of that
Port to cause all such Ships to be strictly visited and
Searched." On December 12 the collector stopped the
Ann of Leith, which had on board, besides her load of
coals, "18 great packs and 14 small Packs of wooll and
4 hogsheads of Combed Wooll For which there was no
Cocquett." Later another vessel with 28 packs of wool
from Leith was seized. The Commissioners recognised
samples of the wool sent them to be English, and ordered
both wool and ships to be taken. But the Attorney General
and Solicitor General decided that though the wool was
forfeit, because it had been exported from England, the
ships were not, as they did not carry it out of England[2].

[1] British Museum, Harl. MSS. 1324, f. 37.
[2] *S. P. Domestic, William III*, iii., Feb. 1698–9.

A certain Frenchman, Toryn by name, seems to have been a great offender in this matter. In 1697 he was living at Wandsworth, but had "for Seven Years last Exported very great Quantities of Wool yearly from Edinburgh in Scotland to Ports beyond the Seas; which Wooll was brought into Scotland out of Northumberland[1]." This Toryn may have been some connection of "Abraham Torin," Protestant refugee from France, who in 1692 was master of the hat manufactory in the Canongate, Edinburgh[2]. The clothiers also complained of this smuggling trade. In January 1697, a petition was presented to the House of Commons from the inhabitants of Ripon, to the effect that the market for wool, which had always been held there twice a week, was "extremely lessened and is in Danger to be lost, for that many People presume to carry their wool into Scotland to the Prejudice of the Northern Woollen Manufactory[3]."

A good deal of information as to the trade and the attempts at prevention is given in a petition, entitled, "The Deplorable Case of the Chief and other Agents or Officers that have been deputed and concerned in the Preventing the Carrying away and the Exportation of the Wool of this Kingdom[4]." Upon the "pressing Solicitations of the Clothiers and Traders in the North parts of this Kingdom, and upon Information, that several Thousand Packs of Wool had been Yearly carryed from thence into Scotland and there shipt off with the Wool of their own Growth to France," some officers were, in

---

[1] *Commons Journals*, xii., p. 176.

[2] *S. P. C. R.*, 5 Jan. 1692.

[3] *Commons Journals*, xii., p. 64.

[4] British Museum, 816 *m.* 14 (89). (c. 1700.)

1698, sent to the north to prevent this trade. There they, "with the Hazard of their Lives, made many Seizures of Wool, to the great Comfort and Rejoicing of Many well meaning Traders." Finding their institution to be attended with so much success in the north, officers were then sent to all the maritime counties, where also they prevented the transportation of much wool. But the officers had spent "the most Part...of their own Substance" in the work, and therefore begged for a "present Supply of Money." They added to their petition some figures to shew the great value of their services. By the export of 30,000 packs of wool, which were in one year landed at three ports in France, His Majesty lost £75,000 customs, and 188,994 people lost a year's employment. Towards the end of the century the Scots cloth manufacturers began to complain of loss to their industry through the export of wool. After some agitation this was forbidden by the Privy Council in 1699, and in 1701 by Parliament[1]. These Acts did not put a stop to the trade, but the amount exported decreased very much. In 1698 it was said that 360,000 stones of wool were sent abroad, chiefly to France. Of this, 170,000 stones were English. In 1700 only 7196 stones were exported, 4503 from England, and in 1704, 4362 stones, including 3091 of English wool[2]. Much controversy between the growers of wool, the merchants and the manufacturers followed. The latter argued that their works could not subsist without a plentiful supply of wool. The growers and exporters declared that there was not a sufficient market

---

[1] *Acts, Scotland*, x., p. 277.

[2] *Essay upon Industry and Trade*, Advocates' Library, Pamphlets, Vol. 505.

for their wool in Scotland, and also that the export of English wool was profitable to the country. "Scotland, by allowing this export may have a considerable Trade in English wool, its an advantage no other nation would have neglected so long[1]." In 1704 the matter was settled by a compromise. "Sheeps wool and Woollen Yearn whither of the grouth of this or any other Kingdom," and also skins with wool on them, might be exported, while the importation of woollen cloth was prohibited, and woollen cloth exported was freed from any impost[2].

After this Act was passed, the smuggling over the border increased. In September 1705, the Commissioners wrote to Godolphin, in reference to a petition to Her Majesty from "ye Merchants Clothiers and other Traders in ye Woolen Manufacture in and about ye Towns of Leeds and Hallifax." In this they complained of "ye Great Decay of their Trade Occasioned by Vast Quantityes of Wooll which are dayly carried into Scotland from ye Counties of Durham, Northumberland and Cumberland and from thence Transported into France and other Forreigne Parts....Ye offenders have Grown so Bold that They come above 50 Miles and Carry Wooll off in Dispite of all Laws." The Commissioners suggest that the three "Ryding Officers" should receive an addition of £20 each to their salaries, with which to pay an assistant, "wch will be a further Encouragement and Security to them in the Discharge of their Duty." They also suggest that all the officers should be provided with fire-arms, "for their Defence against ye Inseults of ye Smuglers...which they

---

[1] *Letter...concerning Manufactures and Trade*, Advocates' Library, Pamphlets, Vol. 349.

[2] *Acts, Scotland*, xi., p. 190.

conceive is all that can be done to Prevent this Clandestine Trade without the assistance of a Military Force[1]." Defoe says that " Scotland freely and openly Exported their Wool to France, Germany and Sweden, to the irreparable Loss of the English Manufactures having great Quantities of English Wool brought into Scotland over the Borders, which it was impossible for England to prevent, so that the Famous Trade for Wool to France by Rumney Marsh, commonly called Owling, was intirely Dropt, and France not Supplyed only, but glutted with Wool[2]."

In the wool trade the unsatisfactory state of the relationship between England and Scotland was particularly evident. England could not control the Scottish Parliament, and could not secure either the prohibition of the export of wool from Scotland, nor the co-operation of the Scots government in preventing the smuggling trade between the two countries. The prospect of securing her own and the Scots supply of wool was one reason which led England to consent to open her Plantation trade to the Scots. They, on their side, had found the English impositions on linen and salt a great hindrance to trade.

c. TRADE WITH IRELAND

During this period there was a good deal of trade and trafficking between the west of Scotland and Ireland, especially with Ulster. A great deal of the trade of the Clyde ports was with Larne, Belfast, Coleraine, London-

---

[1] *Treasury Out-letters, Customs*, XIII., 390.
[2] *History of the Union of England and Scotland*, Defoe, p. 55.

derry and other north of Ireland ports.   From these they
received chiefly provisions, butter, cheese, beef, etc., and
also timber, hides and tallow.   The Scots sent thither
chiefly linen, plaiding, stockings, etc.   The import of Irish
cattle and horses was forbidden in 1667 and 1668[1], and
of " Irish victuell " a few years later.   As usual the
prohibitions were but little regarded, and the Privy
Council books contain records of many prosecutions for
infringement, and of renewed Proclamations for enforcing
the regulations.   Occasionally in time of " dearth and
skaircetie of victuell," the prohibitions were removed,
or licences were given for importing meal, corn, and
other grain.   Licences were also given for importing
horses, and in 1682 this prohibition was removed, as " it
is absolutely necessar for tilleadge and laboureing that
Irish horses be imported[2]."   To facilitate communication
between the countries a horse post was established[3] and
harbours were improved.   There was a considerable emi-
gration of small farmers and servants to Ireland.   In 1678
complaint was made that " sundry tenents and persons of
mean quality have gone over to Ireland...which if not
prevented may tend to the great prejudice of heretors
and others in some places of this kingdome who were
theirby lyke to be left destitut of tenents and servants[4]."
Therefore a licence from the Privy Council was required
before any " tenents—cottars or servants " could be transported to Ireland.

When the exportation of Irish wool and woollen
manufactures to "foreign parts" was prohibited, it was

[1] *S. P. C. R.*, 1 Feb. 1667, 9 Apr. 1688.
[2] *Ibid.*, 8 June 1682.   [3] *Ibid.*, 27 Nov. 1677.
[4] *Ibid.*, 26 March 1678.

feared that the wool would be sent to Scotland, "it being impossible to hinder the Scotch with their broad open boates to carry off in 3 houres from Ireland all the Wooll that Kingdome will supply them with, and when it is in Scotland the Law cannot reach them there and they are att Liberty to carry that Wool to France or to any other Markett[1]." About the same time (1699) another pamphleteer wrote concerning the Scots in Ireland: "that nation has in a great measure engrossed the whole Trade of this Kingdom and a good part of our Lands, and I doubt not but in time they will swallow down all the English Interest here, for they are so nationale that from the Noble to ye pedlar with his Pack they are all Brokers for one another and all the will they have could never have procured them a better handle than ye late English act, for Provoking out ye English here, for one Englishman that has left us we have 6 Scots in his roome[2]." The Act referred to here is that same Act forbidding the transport of Irish wool abroad.

d. TRADE WITH THE PLANTATIONS

One of the principal reasons for Scottish discontent with her English connection during the latter part of the seventeenth century, was her exclusion from the Plantation trade by successive Navigation Acts. Partly excluded as she was from both English and foreign markets, she was anxious to find some demand for her linen and cloth, and her newly-established manufactures. This could only exist in a colonial market, where there were no already

---

[1] British Museum, Additional MSS. 21133, f. 28.
[2] *Ibid.*, f. 45.

established manufactures, and Scotland had no colonies of her own. Her exclusion from the Plantation trade was therefore the most disastrous result of her commercial separation from England after the Restoration. The Act for the Encouraging and increasing of Shipping and Navigation[1] of 1660 declared that no goods should be imported into or exported from his Majesty's dominions in Asia, Africa or America, except in ships belonging to England, Ireland, Wales, Berwick-upon-Tweed, or the Plantations, of which the master and three-fourths of the crew were to be English. No goods of the growth or manufacture of Asia, Africa, or America were to be imported into England, except in English or colonial ships. No foreign goods were to be brought into England, except in English ships or in ships belonging to the country where the goods were produced. Aliens were excluded from the English coasting trade. Certain Plantation commodities, sugar, tobacco, etc., were not to be shipped to any place except England, or the English Plantations.

The Scots merchants at once remonstrated, and threatened to "take the lyk cours with thame," if they were not allowed to retain those privileges which they had had since James VI's accession. No change was made in the English Act, and the Scots Parliament in 1661 passed the Act for Encouraging of Shipping and Navigation[2], which enjoined the use of Scots vessels, or vessels of the country where the goods were produced, and no others, in import trade. All goods exported in foreign ships were to pay double customs. English and Irish ships were excepted, "Provyding alwayes that Scots

[1] 12 Car. II, c. 18.   [2] *Acts*, *Scotland*, vii., p. 257.

vessells enjoy the lyke benefite of trade within the Kingdomes and dominions of England and Ireland." This Act did not cause any concessions to be made, and a few months later the Earls of Glencairne and Rothes, Chancellor and President of the Council in Scotland, petitioned the King that the Act should be declared "not to extend to Y^r Maties subjects in Scotland as being aliens and strangers." They declared that the enforcement of the Act would ruin all trade in Scotland[1]. As a result the Act was suspended as regards Scotland, and the question was referred to a committee consisting of the Lord High Treasurer of England, Lauderdale, Ashley, and others. The Customs Commissioners were requested to make a report to this committee. In this they declared that the admission of the Scots to the trade would be "destructive to ye English Interest prejudiciall to His Matie in his Customes and duties and absolutely pernicious to the Act of Navigation." Their reasons for this decision were given. They feared that the customs would suffer by the Scots paying native customs, which were only half the rate of the aliens' customs they would otherwise pay. They would be able to trade with the Plantations, which "are absolute English." This would enable them to supply continental countries, and to make Scotland a magazine for colonial produce, "and leave us to our home Consumption." They feared also that the Dutch, "against which the Act principally aymes at," would be able to trade under cover of the Scots. Then, if the Scots were allowed to trade as English, they could give no valid security for obeying the regulations of the Act, as the English officials had no control over their

[1] *S. P. Domestic, Charles II*, xl., 104.

property. "They in one word overthrow the very essence
and designe of the Act of Navigation[1]." The Committee,
upon hearing this report, and also interviewing some
merchants and members of the House of Commons, came
to the conclusion that the freedom demanded was "contrary to the main End of the Act of Parliament[2]." The
order suspending the Act was therefore revoked. This
occasioned much complaint from the Burghs, who lamented
that the Act was "totallie destructive to the tread and
navigation of this Kingdome." They said that "a great
pairt of our stockis which wee most send abroad, consistis
of English manufactures which wee most buy for our
money." One difficulty "exceidinglie stood upon" by
the English was "in respect of the great tread at present
with the Barbadoes, and hopes of dryving a richer tread
heirefter with all the Illandis, they intending to plant
synomen, nutmegis cleues and peper, for they have sent
to the East Indies for all these plantis, and they conceauve
that if wee sall have any tread wee willbe able…to undir-
sell thame and furnisch many places of Europe with the
commodities of these plantationis[3]." As matters stood,
Scottish exclusion from the English commercial system
was the inevitable result of the stricter development of
that system after the Restoration. Scotland had her own
Parliament, and the English Parliament had no control
over it nor over Scottish commercial regulations. Her
admission to a share in English trade, therefore, could
be of no direct benefit and might prove injurious to
England. Therefore Scotland was not included in the
English system.

[1] *S. P. Domestic, Charles II*, xliv., 12.   [2] *Ibid.*, 66.
[3] *Royal Burghs*, iii., p. 555.

In 1663 another Act was passed which forbade the import of any goods of the growth, production or manufacture of Europe to the Plantations, except in English ships and shipped in England. Scottish servants, victuals, horses, and also salt were excepted, and might be taken from Scotland, but in English ships. Penalties for infringements were made more severe. The aims of the Navigation Acts were set forth in the preamble. "And in regard His Majesties Plantations beyond the Seas are inhabited and peopled by His subjects of this his Kingdome of England, For the maintaining a greater correspondence and kindnesse betweene them and keepinge them in a firmer dependance upon it, and rendering them yet more beneficiall and advantagious unto it in the farther Imployment and Encrease of English shipping and seamen, Vent of English Woollen and other Manufactures and Commodities...and making this Kingdom a Staple not only of the Commodities of those Plantations but alsoe of the Commodities of other Countryes and Places for the supplying of them[1]." A letter sent from the Treasury to the Governors of the Plantations in 1677, ordering them to enforce the Act, recited this preamble, adding the words, "And for the farther and more peculiar appropriating the trade of these Plantations to the Kingdom of England exclusive from all other His Majesty's dominions[2]." The Plantations were clearly not intended to be "advantagious" to his Majesty's ancient kingdom of Scotland.

The Scots endeavoured to force concessions from England by enforcing their Act of Navigation[3], and by

[1] 15 Car. II, c. 7.　　　　[2] *Treasury Outletters, Customs*, I., 51.
[3] *S. P. C. R.*, 2 Jan. 1662.

laying heavy duties on English imports into Scotland.
These were to be removed as soon as trade with England
was "restored to the condition it was in during the reigne of
his Maiesties father and Grandfather of blessed memorie[1]."
English merchants trading to Scotland were seriously
affected by this Act, and they too petitioned that the
drawbacks on Scottish trade might be removed, but
without any effect. The Council and planters in Barbadoes were also very anxious that the Scots should be
allowed to trade thither. They had supplied the colony
with "braue Seruants and faithfull subiects," who "kept
the Collonys in so formidable a posture, that they neither
feared the Insurrection of their Slaves nor any invasion
from a forreigne Enemy, but are now by the Act of Navigation forbidden to have trade with Scotland; whereby
they can have no servants from thence, and those Scots
now wander into Poland and Germany to serve other
princes which heretofore by their transporting to the
Collonyes did increase the wealth and defend the
Dominions of his Ma[tie][2]."

Charles himself wished the Scots to be allowed to
trade. In 1664 he granted a licence to a certain John
Brown, who had set up sugar-works in Scotland, to trade
to the Plantations with four Scottish ships, as the Scots
"seeme to be excluded" from trading with these parts[3].
To his initiative must be ascribed the negotiations for a
commercial treaty between the two countries which began
in 1668. The Scots insisted that they should consider
"that first and great obstruction of the freedome and
liberty of trade between the two kingdomes, the Act

[1] *Acts, Scotland*, VII., p. 466.   [2] *S. P. Col.*, XXII., 20.
[3] *S. P. Domestic, Charles II, Dom. Entry Book*, XVI., 286—7.

of Navigation," before any other subjects were discussed[1].
On this subject the English were obdurate. The Plantations " were found out, possessed planted and built by the
labour, blood and vast expences of his Ma^{tyes} subiects of
the kingdome of England and doe belong to the Crowne
of England and therefore it cannot be reasonably expected
that Scotland should reape the benefit thereof....And
therefore we cannot allow that the Ships and vessells
of Scotland be permitted this trade[2]." The negotiations
therefore were fruitless, as were those of 1670–1 for a
complete union. It took forty years more to convince
the English that to obtain control of Scottish trade, it
was worth their while to admit the Scots to the English
commercial system.

The Scots seemed now to realise that they could not
hope for any concessions from England, and that if they
wished to have any trade with America it must be carried
on despite the prohibitions. One more licence was granted
(1669), by the influence of the Duke of York. He "did
propose to His Majesty in Councell that hee would bee
pleased to give liberty that such of His Majesty's Subjects
in Scotland as shall bee induced to take condicons as
Planters at New Yorke may bee permitted to transport
themselves thither in vessells from Scotland and bee
allowed to make their voyages and returne in a way of
Trade[3]." Licences were given to two Scots ships to trade
between Scotland and New York. The Commissioners
of the Customs remonstrated at once. They said they
had "cause to believe that tho' their pretensions be very
Smooth and innocent yet the end thereof is to settle a

---

[1] *S. P. Domestic, Charles II*, ccxxxiii., 60.
[2] *Ibid.*, ccxxxvi., 133.   [3] *New York Colonial MSS.*, iii., p. 180.

Trade betwixt ye Plantations and Scotland." Even by
the trade of two ships His Majesty's revenue would lose
"above £7000 per annum[1]."

Some illicit trade had already been carried on by the
Scots, and from about the year 1670 onwards it gradually
increased and became of quite a considerable volume by
the end of the century. The Clyde ports were of course
the most conveniently situated for voyages to America,
but vessels also sailed from Aberdeen and Leith. The
cargoes were chiefly coarse cloth and linen, stockings, hats,
and beef, often brought to Scotland from Ireland, and then
re-exported. The Collector of the Customs in Carolina
wrote in 1687 that the Scots "are evidently able to
undersell ye English, their Goods being either much
Courser or slighter, wch will Serve for Servants weare
and will be sure to go off, they being cheap so that an
Englishman must go away unfreighted or sell to vast
Disadvantage." From the Plantations were received principally tobacco, sugar (for the sugar manufactories at
Glasgow and Leith), and furs and skins. Colonial ships
too came to Scotland, often no doubt the property of Scots
settled in the Plantations.

In Scotland this trade was countenanced by the
authorities. In the colonies it was not so in theory,
though in reality the Customs officials, especially in the
Proprietary colonies, seem to have been very lax. Public
opinion was generally in favour of the illicit traders, at
any rate the officials who were sent out by the home
government at different times, had great difficulty in
obtaining convictions in the courts against those who
infringed the Acts. There were many complaints of this

[1] *New York Colonial MSS.*, iii., p. 181.

kind, from both Randolph and Quary, who were sent from England to look after the collection of the King's customs. The Governor of Maryland, writing to the Committee of Trade and Plantations in 1695, says: "I have found by experience that it is a difficult thing to get Judges and Jurys to try and condemn illegal traders[1]." One or two of the colonies declared that the Acts of Navigation did not bind them and that the English Commissioners of the Customs had no authority there. Randolph wrote from New England in 1690, that he was "alwaies opposed in open Court by the Magistrates and my Seizures and prosecutions (tho made upon very plain Evidence) were ended ineffectual, for the Juries found for the Defendant against His Majesty all agreeing that the Power of the Commissioners of the Customes in matters of Trade did not extend to their Colony[2]." In Carolina the settlers declared that, as they received their charter after the Navigation Acts were passed, they were not in force in that colony. The Collector wrote that some cases were given against him in the courts there. The evidence was not very clear, but "it was declared that, if it had been never so clear they would have pleaded the benefit of their charter...which was granted after the act was passed[3]." Most of the Customs officials were not above reproach: the "Illegal Trade So caryed on...is Connived at and Encouraged by divers of their Maj[ties] Collectors of ye Customes in Virginia etc who are (Underhand) interested and Concerned therein[4]."

[1] S. P. Col., Board of Trade, Maryland, ii., 114.

[2] Ibid., Col. Entry Book, lxii., 231.

[3] Historical Collections of South Carolina, B. R. Carroll, ii., p. 342.

[4] Treasury Papers, xxvi., 53 (1694).

As the American coastline is so long it was of course comparatively easy to evade the authorities altogether, unload in a retired creek, dispose of the goods and obtain a cargo of tobacco, etc. " The inhabitants of the Eastern shore of Virginia, Maryland and Delaware River, Scotchmen and others have great stocks lying by them, to purchase tobacco and to prepare a loading ready to be put on board upon the Arrivall of any Vessell from New England etc, who assist with boats and sloops to get the goods ashoar before the Vessell is Entred, wch they dispose of amongst their goods in the Store, the Vessell lying in some obscure creek 40 or 50 Miles distance from the Collectors office and in a Short time loaded and sailes out of the Capes undiscovered." There were, too, many ways of deceiving the officials. False certificates were much used by the merchants. Some of the collectors " Receive their goods by falce Cocketts wch they know to be made in Glascow and the seales of their Maj^{ties} Commissioners for ye Customs of London and those of several of the outports of England Counterfeited and affixed thereto. Particularly those of Newcastle Berwick Bristoll Beaumorrice Beddeford Whitehaven Liverpoole and Plimouth[1]." The manœuvres of colonial vessels coming from Scotland are described by the Carolina Collector. " The Scotch Trade by the like Legerdemain jugles is driven. A ship at Newcastle Berwick Poole etc toucheth, taketh in coals or some other slight goods, goes for Scotland and there receives great quantities of Linen and other Scotish goods…and coming here by her English clearings at the Ports etc abovesaid passeth for current without further

---

[1] *Treasury Papers*, xxvi., 53 (1694).

inquisition[1]." Randolph, in one of his many letters, gives an account of his experiences in trying to get a conviction for an offence of this nature. He seized two ships which had certificates saying that they had loaded their cargoes of Scots goods at Berwick. He declared that they had been taken on board at Leith and Glasgow, and demanded a court for a trial. "A Scotch Irishman summoned a Jury and returned a Jury of known Scotch and their friends....I proceeded against Makay's Ship for Importing goods not legally shipt in England and proved in Court by the oath of Hugh Moore a Scotch minister passenger in Makay's Ship from Leith to Maryland that they sailed thence towards Berwick. There a Scotchman and master of the ship brought a so-called Customs officer on board who gave a Coquet. One of the Judges told the Court and Jury that they were not to stand upon such Nicetyes ...and the jury brought in verdict for the defendant[2]."

Proposals were made at different times with a view to putting a stop to the illicit trade. It was ordered that more care should be taken in examining certificates and coquets, and in taking bond for observing the Acts, and also that some of the collectors should be removed and "men of integrity" appointed. It was also suggested that several small boats should be chartered to cruise about and discover those ships which unloaded and loaded in secluded bays and creeks. One or two small boats were equipped in accordance with these instructions. One of these was put in command of one Thomas Much, who in 1692 was "an old offender," but in 1694 is found "humbly acknowledging the Unhappy part himself had

[1] S. P. Col., Col. Records of North Carolina, I., 245 (1679).

[2] Ibid., America and West Indies, DCXXXVII., 110.

been unwarily Seduced to act in these misdemeanours," and to shew his remorse "faithfully discovering divers fraudulent and Illegal practise of Severall Scotch merchants[1]." But "notices were given and the Alarm taken on ye Scotch coast," though even so, Much succeeded in taking two ships.

On this side, too, efforts were made to stop the trade. English privateers were sent to cruise about the Scottish coast, especially on the Clyde, to arrest ships trading to America. The Scots merchants naturally objected very strongly to this practice. They were backed up by the Privy Council, which several times wrote to the King complaining of this encroachment on the sovereign rights of Scotland. In 1694 they declared that "both in our East and west Seas and in the ports and harbours therof our merchant ships have been seized...and furder we are Informed that severall other merchant English shipps have taken out Commissions of Mart from the Admiralty against unlawful Traders which we see they mostly make use of against our ships Coming from the plantations. Albeit be certane that before this late warr none of our ships could be attacqued or mollested on that account at sea But onely in the ports and harbours of America....Our merchants are soe much discouradged and prejudged by these attempts that many of them already hes given over trade[2]."

The trade with the Plantations must have been of little importance for the first ten or fifteen years after the Restoration, until the country had had time to recover from the poverty caused by the Civil Wars. What

[1] *Treasury Papers*, xxvi., 53 (1694).
[2] *S. P. C. R.*, 29 June 1694.

trade there was during these years was chiefly with Barbadoes, but from about the year 1676 until the Union, there are many complaints about the Scots trade with the Plantations. A considerable number had settled in different colonies and they naturally kept up communication with Scotland, and assisted their countrymen in trade. In 1682 an Admiralty official in New Hampshire wrote, "There are severall Scotsmen that inhabit here, and are great Interlopers, and bring in quantities of goods underhand from Scotland[1]." Again : "Somerset county in Maryland is pestered with Scotch and Irish." Some of the Council are Scots, and "support ye Interlopers and buy up all their loading upon first arrivall and govern ye whole trade on ye Eastern shore so that whereas 7 or 8 good ships from England did yearly Trade and load ye Tobb° of that Colony I find that in these 3 years past there has not been above 5 ships trading legally in all these Rivers" (Delaware and other Maryland rivers) "and nigh 30 sayle of Scotch Irish and New England Men[2]." The Custom House officials had agents in Scotland from whom they received notice as to trade. In "Commercial Orders to Governor Andros" they write (1687), "We are frequently informed from our agents in Scotland of several ships coming thither with the innumerated Plantation commodities without touching to clear in any port of England Wales or Berwick[3]." Boston was a great centre for illegal trade and Boston ships often went to Scotland. In October 1689 three were said to be in Scotland while three others had just left[4].

[1] *S. P. Col., Col. Papers*, L., 3.

[2] *Ibid., America and West Indies*, DCXXXVII., 110.

[3] *Massachusetts Historical Society Collections*, VII. and VIII., p. 175.

[4] *S. P. Col., Col. Entry Book*, LXII., 240.

During William's wars with France illegal trade with America seems to have increased. Davenant says that " during this war, the colonists have presumed...to set up for themselves, and to load their effects in ships belonging to foreigners and to trade directly with other nations, sending them their commodities and receiving from thence manufactures not of our growth to the great damage of this kingdom[1]." The number of English ships trading to the colonies decreased. The Governor of Virginia in 1695 begged that " a good number of ships be permitted to come to these parts for when few come then goods are very dear and tobacco very cheap[2]." Scottish ships took advantage of the opportunity given by English difficulties and colonial necessities, and their trade during the years 1690–1695 increased considerably. But they did not wholly escape the French privateers. In 1694 a Glasgow merchant wrote that he had for " several years bypast driven ane considerable trade to the West Indies by exporting the native product of this Kingdom and Importing from thence Tobacco Suggar and other Commodities of these Countries Bot since the present wars with ffrance, the petitioner hes sustained great Loss by the privateers of that natione viz. £1300 sterling in the Mary of St Marys laden with tobacco and sugar taken within 48 hours of New Port Glasgow, £600 tobacco in Plain Dealing of Coleraine £306 dry goods in Success of Boston outwards bound £780 in Mary of Boston homewards bound £39. 1Q. 6 in Mary of Bo'ness outward with dry goods Total £3013. 10." He also lost a ship laden

---

[1] *History of the Revolt of the American Colonies*, G. Chalmers, I., p. 269.

[2] *S. P. Col.*, *Board of Trade*, Maryland, II., 114.

with tobacco, which was seized by the English privateers[1].
In the year 1693–1694 thirteen ships loaded by Scots
merchants arrived in Virginia and Maryland. Their
cargoes were rum, sugar, linen, and "Scotch Goods," and
they loaded there with tobacco, nine sailing to Scotland,
and one to Holland[2]. The destination of the other three
was doubtful. A list of fourteen Glasgow merchants who
traded with the Plantations was given by Much in 1695[3],
and he said there were several others whose names he
had forgotten. The agent of the English Customs Commissioners in Scotland gave a list of the ships trading
between Scotland and the Plantations between 15 April
1695 and 29 December 1696, twenty-seven in all[4]. They
were chiefly Scottish ships, bringing tobacco from Virginia
and Maryland, and taking out "Scotch Goods." Scots
merchants also traded between the English colonies and
the Dutch possessions of Surinam and Curaçoa. "Severall
Scotch merchants in Pennsilvania...cary the Tobacco of
Maryland to Surenham and Carressoe in bread Casks
covered with flower at each end[5]."

About this time merchants in England began to complain very much of the Scottish trade. The Customs House
officers of Liverpool wrote in 1692 that they had received
many complaints from merchants and masters of ships,
that "not only their Majesties Revenue is much lessened
but themselves and all others both Merchants and Masters
of Ships who Lawfully Trade to the said Plantacons much

---

[1] *Customs and Foreign Excise, Tacksmen's Accompts*, Vol. VII.

[2] *S. P. Col., Board of Trade*, Virginia, V., 66.

[3] *Ibid., Board of Trade*, Maryland, III., 2.

[4] *H. M. C. R., House of Lords MSS.*, II., p. 464.

[5] *S. P. Col., Board of Trade*, Maryland, VIII., 188 (1695).

discouraged and almost ruined by reason their Majesties officers in the Plantations...do...Corruptly or unfairly comply with Persons treading from Scotland...as also others from New England who Sail directly to Scotland with their Plantation goods and discharge there[1]." The London merchants also declared that "their Trade is in a great Measure destroyed and ruined by many ships Trading directly from Scotland and Ireland to Virginia Maryland and Pennsylvania And from thence back to the said Places[2]." The Bristol traders sent a petition to the House of Commons complaining of the same prejudice to their trade in 1694[3].

The feeling against Scotland and Scottish interlopers was strengthened by the Act of 1695, constituting the "Company of Scotland, Trading to Africa and the West Indies." The officials in America regarded it as an attempt to legalise and extend that illicit trade with Scotland which they had been endeavouring to suppress. The Commissioners of the Customs declared themselves "humbly apprehensive of this growing mischief, for ye Trade between Scotland and the Plantations is now about to be more openly carried on under Colour of a Law lately passed in Scotland[4]." Until 1696 the administration of the Acts had been comparatively lax, but after that date it became far more stringent, as did the supervision of the colonial officials. A new Board of Trade and Plantations was erected, and Admiralty courts were set up in the colonies. This general tightening up of the code was

[1] *S. P. Col.*, *Board of Trade*, Bermudas, xxviii., pp. 41—45.

[2] *Ibid.*, *Board of Trade*, Virginia, v., 46. i. (1694.)

[3] *Commons Journals*, xi., p. 188.

[4] *S. P. Col.*, *Col. Entry Book*, c., 352.

the result of the Act of 1696. This was passed partly to guard against any danger that might arise from the Scots Act of 1695, but chiefly in consequence of the many petitions, complaints and remonstrances regarding the Plantation trade. The "Act for preventing Frauds and regulating Abuses in the Plantation Trade[1]" recited all the provisions of Charles II's statutes relating to colonial trade, asserted their validity in all the Plantations, ordered the governors and officers to take oaths for the proper performance of their duties, and made the administration of the Acts generally far more stringent. Special reference was made to the Scottish trade: "And whereas great Frauds and Abuses have beene committed by Scotch men and others in the Plantation Trade by obtruding false and counterfeite Certificates upon the Governors and Officers in the Plantations...whereof they may carry the Goods of Scotland and other Places of Europe without Shipping or lading the same in England ...to His Majesty's Plantations and also carry the Goods of the Plantations directly to Scotland, or to any Market in Europe without bringing the same to England." Greater care was therefore to be taken in examining certificates, accepting security, etc.

Notwithstanding the provisions of this new Act, and the fact that a great deal of the capital of the Scottish nation was engaged in the Darien scheme, the trade with the Plantations still continued. In 1701 Quary wrote from Pennsylvania, that "Four times the Quantity of tobacco was made there that year than had been made there before, and all of it engrossed by the Scotch as

[1] 7 & 8 Gul. III, c. 22.

almost all other trade there was[1]." Two or three years later there was a good deal of discussion about the advisability of allowing the export of Irish linen to the Plantations. There was some fear that it might lead also to a free export of Scots linen: "when the Linnen of Ireland should have so direct a Current to ye Plantacons I believe it will be impossible to hinder an Indraught of Scotch Linnen too into Ireland, from whence It may be carried directly to America." The Customs Commissioners were against permission being given for the export, but it was finally allowed. At the same time however the export of Scots linen into Ireland was prohibited[2]. The spirit of this Act was shewn in the negotiations for union, in the reluctance of England to grant freedom of trade to the Plantations. But that concession was of the greatest importance to the Scots, and it was finally granted. At the same time England obtained the power of parliamentary regulation of that trade to the west which the Scots merchants had built up in spite of prohibitions, restraints, and many difficulties.

e. Settlement in America

Scottish trade with America was facilitated and encouraged by the immigration of settlers from Scotland, who were doubtless anxious to keep up a connection with the mother country. Large numbers were sent over during the Commonwealth period, especially after the battles of Dunbar and Worcester. In New England at any rate they seem to have been well treated. A letter to Cromwell from that colony says that "we have been

---

[1] *Treasury Papers*, LXXIII., 43. [2] 3 & 4 A., c. 7.

anxious, as far as we could, to make their yoke easy....
They have not been sold for slaves to perpetual servitude,
but for 6 or 7 or 8 years...and he that bought most of
them buildeth houses for them...and promiseth that as
soon as they can repay him the money laid out for them
he will set them at liberty[1]." Many of these, having
served their time as servants, settled down, and became
prosperous planters or merchants. The settlers in New
Jersey found many of them when they went over in 1683,
having "purchased notable plantations for themselves,
both in Barbadoes Maryland and else-where and live very
plentifully accounting themselves happy in that providence
that brought them there, and extremely regrating the
Condition of many of their friends at home, and wishing
them Sharers of their prosperitie." After the Restoration,
and all through the latter part of the century many others
went of their own free will to seek their fortunes in
America and in the Indies. As colonists, and as servants,
they were highly appreciated. In Barbadoes they formed
an important element of the population. When the
settlement of St Lucia was under consideration, it was
suggested that Scots should be allowed to come, as they
would "strengthen the place well, besides they are hardy
people to endure labour and have been the cheif instruments of bringing Barbadoes to it's perfection[2]." It was
thought desirable, too, in Jamaica, that "all prudentiall
means bee used to encourage ye Scotts to come hither as
being very good Seruants[3]." In Virginia, also, the Governor
found them useful settlers. He wrote in 1666 to Lord
Arlington at the "sollicitation of some Scotch Gents,"

---

[1] *Hutchinson Papers* (Prince Society), ii., p. 264.
[2] *S. P. Col.*, *Col. Papers*, xxv., 77. i.   [3] *Ibid.*, 591. ii.

begging leave for them to settle there, as "in this dangerous time they have been very useful to us[1]."

A number also were transported because their presence was unwelcome at home. His Majesty's Plantations were a dumping ground for "strong and idle beggars vagabonds Egiptians common and notorious theives and other dissolut and lous persones banished or stigmatised for grosse crymes." Although persons thus designated would not seem to be very desirable members of a community, there was a great demand for their services in America, and merchants and ship masters found them a very profitable commodity to export. In fact people were often kidnapped and taken off to the Plantations. The Privy Council frequently gave orders to search ships "bounding" for America, "and if they find any persons yr who are not of their owne consent and freewill content to be caryed to the said plantations or are not condemned yrto by ye sentence of a judge That they bring them a shore and dismiss them[2]." Of the "vagabonds" it was said that "severall persones so sent away within these 9 or 10 years have become very active and virtuous persones Their idleness and poverty having formerly corrupted them[3]." Another class of persons transported were "obstinat phanaticks" and "absenters from the church." The Council was anxious to "empty the prisons and be ride of thos vermine," and numbers were sent to America, generally to Virginia, Maryland, Barbadoes or the Caribbee Islands. A number of Presbyterians also emigrated on their own account. As early as 1680 there were Scottish Presbyterian meeting houses and congregations in

[1] S. P. Col., Col. Papers, xx., 185.
[2] S. P. C. R., 5 Aug. 1668.   [3] Ibid., 16 Aug. 1680.

Virginia, Maryland and also in New Jersey[1], even before part of the colony came under the Scottish proprietors. Some of the members of these congregations were from Ulster, descendants of the Scottish colonists there. In Maryland about seven hundred of these Scottish-Irishmen settled between 1685 and 1695. They began linen and woollen manufactures, which were strongly objected to by the authorities, as they feared that they would in time supply the colonies, and thus destroy the market for English manufactures. There were also Scots settlers scattered about in New Hampshire, Pennsylvania and New York.

The Scots, besides settling amongst the English in different parts of the country, made two attempts to found settlements of their own, in New Jersey and in Carolina. New Jersey was granted by Charles to the Duke of York in 1665, and he granted the country to Lord Berkeley and Sir George Carteret. The eastern part, Carteret's share, was later (1682) vested in twenty-four proprietors, who possessed all powers of government and jurisdiction. Twelve of these were Scotsmen, the Earl of Perth, Drummond, Treasurer Depute, Mackenzie, Lord Register, and others, lairds, merchants and advocates[2]. One of their number, Gavin Lawrie, was made governor[3], and instructions were given that all land surveyed should be divided into two parts, one to be for the Scots proprietors[4]. Plans were made for laying out a town at Amboy Point, to be called Perth, and to be the capital of the province. The

[1] *History of the Presbyterian Church in America*, Webster.
[2] *Grants Concessions and Original Constitutions of the Province of New Jersey.*
[3] *New Jersey Colonial Documents*, i., p. 425.   [4] *Ibid.*, p. 446.

country was not unoccupied at this time, the population amounting to about 5000, some in townships and villages, and others scattered about the country. These settlers were principally English, but there were also some Scots and Irish, chiefly Presbyterians in search of religious freedom.

The proprietors in Scotland at once began to try and raise an interest in the project, and to induce settlers to emigrate. They published in 1683 *A Brief Account of the Province of East New Jersey in America*, "for the information of such as may have a Desire to Transport themselves or their families thither." In this pamphlet the country was described, and the advantages of colonies to Scotland were pointed out. Settlement in America was a better means of ridding the country of its superfluous population than allowing them to wander to the Continent, and to serve in foreign armies. Younger sons especially were "forced to go abroad upon their Shifts or hange upon the Laird in a most slavish and sordide manner." The advantage which the colony would afford Scotland as a market for her woollen and linen cloths was pointed out, even though the Navigation Acts were in force there. The plantation products were to be brought to England, and the money got for them there was to be spent in buying Scottish commodities to be exported, which would make "a Circulation of Trade as Advantagious for us, yea more than if returns came straight home." Special licence was given in the charter for transporting settlers and everything necessary for their use from any of his Majesty's dominions. Information was also given about the terms on which land could be acquired. Large estates could be purchased at £100 per

500 acres. Also, the town of Perth was to be divided into lots of 10 acres at £20 each. Husbandmen providing themselves with stock could get from 100 to 500 acres at 2s. 6d. per acre. Servants after four years' service were to receive 25 acres, with "as much Corne as will sow an acre and a sute of new Cloaths." Quite a number availed themselves of this opportunity of settling in a new country. The prospect of religious freedom doubtless was an inducement to many. Those who, "upon account of their not going that length in conformity required of them by the Law, do live very uneasie," found that "besides the other agreable accomodations of that place many there freely enjoy their own principles, without hazard or the least trouble." Ships sailed from Leith, Aberdeen and Montrose, with persons of all classes, proprietors, those who had purchased large estates, ministers, husbandmen, tradesmen, servants. The voyage generally took from six to eight weeks. It was said to be less dangerous than crossing to Holland, but in any case the long confinement in close quarters must have been most tedious and unpleasant. Several would-be settlers indeed died on the voyage. The discomforts of the journey over, they seemed to find the new country all that had been promised. Extracts from letters of settlers are given in a pamphlet published in 1685, "The Model of the Government of the Province of East-New-Jersey in America And Encouragements of such as Designs to be Concerned there[1]." "I have great reason to thank God that I am in a place which abundantly answers anything I expected." "This country is beyond not only all our Expectations but all

[1] *East Jersey under the Proprietary Government*, W. A. Whitehead, p. 365.

that ever you have heard spoken of it." The Indians were
found to be "a harmless people and very kind to us; they
are not a hairie people as was said to us in Scotland."
One writer enumerates the occupations which may be
followed. "In ¦the first place Planting...in the second
place there may be Fishing...in the third place for one to
have a Malthouse, a brew house and a bake house, to
make malt, brew bear and bake bisket for Barbadoes and
the Neighbouring Colonies;...Lastly for one to buy up the
product of the countrey...and export them to Barbadoes,
and import Rumme and Molasses would certainly be a
good trade in Amboy, for the highest designe of the old
Buckskin Planters (I am just now drinking to one of them,
our Countryman, who was sent away by Cromwell to New
England, a slave from Dunbar, Living now in Woodbridge
Like a Scots Laird, wishes his Countrymen and Native
Soyle very well, tho' he never intends to see it. Pardon
this Parenthesis) is to acquire a piece of money to drink
in the change house." Unlike the "Buckskin Planters,"
the new settlers felt most the "need of good and Faithful
Ministers." One gay youth, however, brother of the Laird
of Kinnaber, hoped that "in a little time I shall want
nothing but the company of the prettie Girls, to all whom
who retain any remembrance of me, Let my services be
remembered."

The infant colony received all encouragement from
Charles and James, but its neighbours soon began to
trouble the settlers. The Governor of New York was
anxious to bring New Jersey under his control[1]. The
Proprietors in 1684 asserted their rights of "Government,
Ports, and Harbours, free Trade and Navigation," and laid

[1] *New Jersey Colonial Documents*, I., p. 463.

the matter before the Duke, whom they found "verie just." Dongan, the New York Governor, however, still continued to trouble them, especially by asserting that Perth Amboy was not a port of entry, and that all vessels trading in that part of the country must enter at New York[1]. He also seized some ships, and forced them to discharge there. The Proprietors declared that they had "adventured great Stocks upon that Bottom," and had sent "several hundred persons out of Scotland," and should therefore be encouraged. They got their way and New Perth was erected into a port of entry in 1687[2]. Naturally it was a favourite resort of Scots ships and merchants.

The population seems to have been divided into two factions, English and Scottish. The latter were encouraged by the appointment of a Scottish Governor, Andrew Hamilton, in 1692, "a great favourer of the Scotch traders his countrymen." But in 1697, as a result of the Act of 1696 which was held to prevent all Scots from holding positions of public trust, Hamilton was dismissed[3], although the Proprietors were most anxious to retain his services. The Attorney-General declared, however, that "a Scotchman borne is by Law capable of being appointed Governor of any one of the Plantacons he being a natural born subject of England in Judgement and Construccon of Law[4]," and Hamilton was restored in 1699[5]. Jeremiah Basse, who had been Governor in the interval, had had great difficulties with the Scots, partly because of his "discountenancinge the Scoch and pirates in their illegall trades." Another reason was his issue of a Proclamation

[1] *New Jersey Colonial Documents*, I., pp. 524, 533.
[2] *Ibid.*, I., p. 535.   [3] *Ibid.*, II., pp. 176, 249.
[4] *Ibid.*, p. 250.   [5] *Ibid.*, p. 301.

forbidding intercourse with the settlers of the Darien
expedition. "The Scotch gentlemen amongst us," he says,
"are growne to a very great hight from the prospect of a
Gentleman of their own Nation filleinge the seat of
Government in these provinces…and the Success that
their Countreymen meet withall in their settlement of…
Golden Island…I cannot see but that the English interest
and trade must of necessity fall if some Spedy course be
not taken for their Stopeinge of their Groath. The
principal traders in East and West Jersey and Pennsilvania are Scotch who some of them have publiquely
asserted that his Majesty dare not interrupt them in their
settlement of Golden Island lest It should make a breach
betwixt the two Nations publiquely[1]." Basse complained
later about Hamilton's reinstalment, declaring that the
"whole designe and end of the Act of 1696" was to
"Keepe the trade of the Plantations intirely in a dependance on England and the great cause of making itt being
the Continued Complaints of an Illegal trade Carried on
by Scotchmen to Scotland Holland Curasoe etc and
connived att by such as are in Authority[2]." Quary, the
Customs Commissioner, reported that in the eastern
division of New Jersey the Scots "by means of the Scotch
Governor Carry things here with a high hand and irritate
the People against them[3]." The population increased
considerably after the Scots settlement, colonists coming
both from England and from Scotland. The English
gradually outnumbered the Scots and were therefore dis-
contented with the proprietary government, under which
the Scots "had the sole rule." This form of government

[1] *New Jersey Colonial Documents*, II., p. 288.
[2] *Ibid.*, p. 420.   [3] *Ibid.*, III., p. 13.

was not considered in any of the colonies to be conducive to
the best results, either for the settlers or for the sovereign,
and New Jersey was no exception to the rule. Indeed the
Scots influence there made the system still more unpopular
with the English authorities. From 1699 to 1702 negotiations were being carried on with a view to the surrender
of the government to the crown, and in 1702 it was finally
given up[1]. In the next year Hamilton died, and Lord
Cornbury was appointed governor.

The Carolina settlement did not meet with as much
success as the New Jersey colony. Sir John Cochrane
and Sir George Campbell were the promoters of this
effort[2], and bought some land from the proprietors of
Carolina in 1682. They intended the settlement to be a
refuge for those who suffered under the Stewarts' ecclesiastical policy. They were therefore anxious to secure
liberty when they emigrated, and insisted on some alterations being made in the constitution. These, however,
were soon repealed, because they were "injudicious and
inapplicable." The land granted to them was to be some
distance inland, to prevent surprises from an enemy, some
distance from the nearest English settlement, and also to
be in a healthy situation, and well provided with water[3].
Lord Cardross and several Scots families went across in
1683, and the settlement was made at Port Royal. Next
year they were joined by other settlers.

Unfortunately the colony got into difficulties, both
with the English settlers and government, and with the
Indians and Spaniards. The English seem to have been

---

[1] *East Jersey under the Proprietary Government*, p. 212.

[2] *S. P. C. R.*, 30 Nov. 1682.

[3] *S. P. Col., Col. Entry Book*, xxi., 129.

jealous of the Scots having anything to do with the
administration of justice, and the Scots resented any
encroachments on what they considered were their un-
doubted rights. A quarrel began over the arrest of a
Scotsman, on "Scotch precints," by English officials. Some
reprisal was made by the Scots and then Lord Cardross
was ordered to appear before the Council. On his neglect
of the summons, a warrant was issued against him for
contempt[1]. The English Proprietors disapproved of this
conduct towards Lord Cardross, and wrote apologising to
him[2]. Cardross, however, returned to Scotland. Before
he left it was said that the Scots had incited a neighbouring tribe of Indians to fall upon another tribe who were
under Spanish protection. The Spaniards thereupon
attacked the Scots settlement and destroyed it, in 1686[3],
when the colony had only been in existence for four years.
Those who escaped settled elsewhere amongst the English
settlers, and no more attempts were made to form an
exclusively Scottish settlement.

A question of some importance throughout this period,
was that of the naturalisation and denisation of the Scots.
The English Navigation Acts declared that ships must be
sailed by crews which were two-thirds English. Although
Scotsmen had been naturalised in England since James VI's
reign, yet it was now asserted that for the purposes of the
Acts Scotsmen could not be considered Englishmen.
The Acts also declared that only Englishmen could be
merchants or factors in the Plantations, and on this point
too the Scots were sometimes challenged. There was much

---

[1] *S. P. Col.*, *Board of Trade*, North Carolina, i., 36.

[2] *Ibid.*, *Col. Entry Book*, xxii., 70, 109.

[3] *Ibid.*, xxi., 140; xxii. 121; xli., 155.

difference of opinion on the subject, and the distinction was not always insisted on. The Scots resented very much any attempts to enforce the Acts in this strict sense. One instance is given in 1669 of a ship which was confiscated at Barbadoes, because some of the necessary English proportion of the crew were Scotsmen. They had paid customs and got coquets in England and "'tis said that diuers of these Scottsmen dwell in England, and did engadge with the hazard of their Lives in the last warres against the Dutch in His Majesty's service who take it wondrous unkindly to be thus debarred the Liberty of subjects." The Barbadoes people considered it "a thing of much rigour" that the Scots should be thus excluded[1]. After a few years, however, it was decided that Scots might navigate English ships[2]. Also, although no legal opinion seems to have been given on the subject, Scots were allowed to be merchants and factors in the colonies. The Act of 1696, which ratified and made more severe the former Acts dealing with navigation, again gave rise to much discussion on these points. One clause declared that places of trust in Courts of Law or Treasury were to be held only by natives of England, Ireland, or the Plantations; also that in cases concerning the infringement of the Acts the jurors should be natives of England, Ireland, or the Plantations only. Under this Act Hamilton, Governor of New Jersey, was dismissed, but was reinstated again in 1699[3]. The Attorney-General and Solicitor-General decided that all Scotsmen "are qualified to be owners, Masters and Mariners of ships in these parts[4]."

[1] S. P. Col., Col. Papers, xxv., 17.
[2] Historical Collections of South Carolina, ii., p. 342.
[3] See above, p. 135.
[4] S. P. Col., Board of Trade, Proprietaries, xxv., 243—47.

They declared also that the words Englishman or native-born subjects of England included Scotsmen[1]. Nevertheless in many cases the colonial authorities disregarded these decisions. A pamphlet published in 1703 declares that "of late years Scotsmen have been very ill-treated in some of the Plantations, such of them as were Justices of the Peace, Members of the Council, or in any other publick office, were turn'd out: Scotsmen residing there have had their Goods and Ships, seized and confiscated, and in many cases they have been proceeded against as Aliens, and forc'd to sell their ships to avoid these Vexations[2]." The interpretation of the Acts probably varied in different colonies, but the position of Scots merchants, planters and seamen alike, was both uncertain and unsatisfactory, and they were all doubtless anxious for union, to obtain equal rights with the English as traders and as settlers.

f. Trade with France

The only new feature of any importance in Scottish trade during this period was the development of the trade to America. There was also some trade to the West Indies, not only to the British islands, but also to the Dutch possessions of Curaçoa and Antigua, and to the Caribbee Islands and St Christopher's. This trade was chiefly carried on by ships from the Clyde ports, which also went to the Canary Islands. But the principal trade of the country was still with Spain, France, Holland, Norway,

---

[1] *Political Annals of the Present United Colonies*, G. Chalmers, I., p. 260.

[2] *The Case of Scotsmen residing in England and in the English Plantations*, Advocates' Library, Pamphlets, Vol. 349.

Sweden, Denmark and the Baltic ports. The towns which the Scots merchants frequented were San Sebastian and Bilbao; Lisbon; Bordeaux, Rochelle, Rouen and Dieppe; Campvere, Middelberg, Rotterdam and Amsterdam; Bergen, Gothenberg and Stockholm; Königsberg, Stettin, Lubeck, Dantzig and Hamburg. The east coast ports had some trade with London, and also with Newcastle, but apart from these there was little trade with England by sea. Between Ireland, especially the north, and the west coast of Scotland, there was much communication.

The Scots still continued to trade in what the English despised as a "mean and peddling" manner. Ships were loaded by a number of merchants, each making some small contribution to the cargo. One man would put on board five hundred pounds of butter; another, one thousand ells of linen cloth and ten dozen stockings; a third, fifty-two kidskins, or five dozen salt hides, or perhaps eight hundred-weight of old brass; and so the ship's load was gradually made up. The ships, too, were sailed more cheaply than English ships. Trade was still much hampered by the special position of the royal burghs, which, in spite of opposition and agitation from the "unfree" burghs, continued to retain their privileges.

Scotland during this period felt the disadvantage of her connection with England far more heavily than she had during the earlier part of the century. Then she had shared in the English coasting trade, and also, though to a small extent, she had traded between England and some continental ports. The Navigation Acts cut her off from all share in either of these branches of trade, as well as from any legitimate share in the Plantation trade. But it was in her foreign trade, rather than in her trade

with England herself, that her English connection was
most disastrous. England's enemies were not Scotland's
enemies, yet because of their common sovereign Scotland
had to share in England's wars. Unfortunately these were
waged against Scotland's friends and commercial allies,
the Dutch, during nearly ten years of Charles's reign; and
the French, during practically the whole of William's
reign. From the Dutch war the Scots suffered in two
ways, from the embargo placed on their trade with
Holland, which was of great importance to them; and
from the damage to their ships sailing to France and the
south from Dutch men-of-war and privateers. During the
long wars with France the state of affairs was somewhat
different. Trade with France was not always prohibited,
and the prohibition was very generally disregarded. But
those who continued to trade suffered both from French
privateers and from English ships, which attempted to
prevent communication between Scotland and France.

Scottish trade with France was injured by the general
commercial conditions in Europe, as well as by her English
connection. During the seventeenth century, especially
in the latter half, both England and France developed
highly protective systems. Scotland was not included in
the English system, and French protection led to the
abolition of her old privileges there. For this the Scots
blamed their relationship with England. They were
greatly disappointed that they were neither represented,
nor their interests considered, at the Treaty of Ryswick,
and that the opportunity was not taken for re-establishing
them in their favoured position in France. There was a
general feeling amongst all classes that this subordination
of their interests could not continue. "There is no

Nation so much hurt in Trade by England as is Scotland;
Because we are under their Head, but not of their
Politick Body....Why do wee loss the Friendship of all
our ancient Allyes for the quarrels betwixt them and
England, whilst England gives neither Friendship free
Trade nor priviledge to us[1]."

At the beginning of the eighteenth century steps
were taken to take the control of foreign relations from
the hands of the sovereign, who was presumably influenced
by English interests, and to make it a national business.
An overture for an Act appointing Scottish residents
and consuls, "in such Places as are most proper for the
trade of this nation," was brought forward[2]. An Act was
passed rescinding the Act of Charles II's first Parliament
which vested in the King the power of ordering foreign
trade, as being "prejudiciall to the Trade of this Nation[3]."
An Act was also brought forward for making the kingdom
a free port, by removing all duties on imports and exports
whether carried by natives or by foreigners[4]. This however was not passed. The Act of Peace and War and the
Act allowing the import of foreign wines were more
important[5]. The former placed the power of declaring
war in the hands of the Scottish Parliament, so that
Scotland need not necessarily be at war with the same
countries as England. The "Wine Act" followed the
same policy; allowing the import of wines legalised trade
with France, while England was still at war with her.
These Acts, shewing that Scotland was going to regulate

[1] *Parainesis Pacifica, or A Perswasive to the Union of Britain.*
[2] *Acts, Scotland,* x., p. 248.   [3] *Ibid.,* p. 275.
[4] *Parliamentary Papers,* xviii., 58.
[5] *Acts, Scotland,* xi., pp. 107, 112.

her own foreign political and commercial relations in her
own interests, naturally alarmed English statesmen, and
did much to force on the Union.

In spite of these drawbacks to her commerce, Scottish
shipping increased somewhat during this period. Under
the Commonwealth the Scots lost most of their ships,
many being taken by the English, while others were lost
during the Dutch wars. In 1662 the Burgh Convention
declared that "in the yeiris 1650 and 1651, and thairefter
the Inglish did sease upon and tak the whole schippis of
Scotland great and small, so that the whole schippis now
belonging to Scotland ar of ane verie inconsiderable value[1]."
The vessels bought after the Restoration were chiefly of
foreign build, very few ships being as yet built in Scotland.
This was another reason against the admission of Scots
ships to share in English commerce[2]. During the Dutch
and French wars the Scots succeeded in capturing some
ships from the enemy, but they also lost a considerable
number. In 1656 the number of ships belonging to the
principal ports was estimated at 127, their total tonnage
being 3866 tons[3]. An inquiry was made into the condition
of the Royal Burghs in 1693[4], and from statements then
made it seems that they owned about 117 ships, but in
this list no Fife, Forth or Clyde ports were given, except
Kirkcaldy, Leith, Queensferry and Glasgow. Aberdeen
too was omitted. Further information was given in a
register of Scottish ships drawn up in 1712[5], in which

[1] *Royal Burghs*, iii., p. 555.
[2] *S. P. Domestic, Charles II*, ccxxxiii., 13.
[3] Tucker's *Report on the Customs and Excise*.
[4] *Royal Burghs*, iii., pp. 563—667.
[5] British Museum, Harleian MSS. 1324.

those put on the register at the time of the Union were specially distinguished. These numbered 215, with a tonnage of 14,485 tons. This list was more exhaustive than either of the others, but there was doubtless some increase in numbers, and certainly a considerable increase in the tonnage of the ships. The Scots employed a number of foreign ships, chiefly Dutch. After the Union they were of course limited to Scottish and English ships, which partly accounts for the growth in shipping in the years 1707–1712, when the increase in the number of Scottish owned ships was 908. This was also due to an increase of trade, and especially to the Scots admission to the Plantation trade. In the Clyde ports, which were most affected by that liberty, the number of ships rose from 21 to 216, a much greater proportional increase than that of any other group of ports.

During the latter part of the century England realised that France was her most formidable rival, both politically and commercially. At the same time she gradually came to recognise the danger of the Scottish connection with France, and the necessity for getting the power to control Scottish relations with foreign powers. France, first under Richelieu, then under the great commercial minister Colbert, began in the seventeenth century to develop her great internal resources, and to consider the interests of trade and industry to be of primary importance. As reprisal for the English Navigation Act, to act as a check to Holland, and also to encourage French shipping, a tax of 50 sous per ton was in 1659 imposed on all foreign vessels trading with France. This imposition was one of the first steps towards building up that complete system of protection which was identified with the name of its

K.   10

originator, Colbert. In 1662, the Dutch Ambassador at Paris wrote to his government, " On remue ciel et terre ici pour ôter aux étrangers la navigation et le commerce[1]." The policy was continued by a new tariff enforced in 1664. This increased the duties on English manufactures, but in 1667 another tariff was enforced, in which the duties upon English and Dutch manufactures were doubled[2]. English merchants were much alarmed, and asserted that trade with France was carried on at a loss of about a million pounds a year. The Whig party took up their cause, and after much agitation a Bill was passed in 1678 entirely prohibiting trade with France[3]. This policy was continued at the Revolution, when English, especially Whig, hatred of France was increased by Louis XIV's great schemes of political aggrandisement, and by his shelter of the exiled Stewarts.

Scotland at this time was placed in a position of great difficulty. England and France were both developing strong protective systems. England had prohibited her trade with the Plantations, and high tariffs in both countries hindered trade between England and Scotland. But her French trade had always been of more importance to Scotland than her English, and her merchants had for long enjoyed special privileges there. They were exempted for four years from the duty on shipping imposed in 1659, but in 1663 it was levied on Scottish ships also. This occasioned many complaints from Scots mer-

---

[1] P. Clément, *Histoire du Système Protecteur en France*, p. 13.

[2] *Ibid.*, pp. 16, 17.

[3] See W. J. Ashley, *Economic Surveys*, *The Tory Origin of Free Trade*; and W. Cunningham, *Growth of English Industry and Commerce in Modern Times*, Vol. ii., p. 458.

chants. They declared that they were "in hazard to be reduced to the common condition of strangers and to losse the benefite of those antient privileges which for many ages they have enjoyed[1]." Her trade with France was so important that she could not afford to make any retaliation, and merely confined herself to complaints and remonstrances, which were futile. Her connection with England was blamed as the cause of her disabilities in France. The difficulty of Scotland's position increased between the Revolution and the Union of the Kingdoms. Politically she was bound up with England, where the King, the powerful Whig party, and most of the mercantile interest were hostile to, and shortly to be at war with France. Commercially she was separated from England by high tariffs and by the Navigation Acts, while the continuance of her trade with France was necessary for her prosperity. There was also a strong party in Scotland who still considered themselves subjects of the exiled King, and who kept up a constant correspondence with the court at St Germain. During the period from the Revolution to the Union, occupied as it was by England's wars with France, Scotland was torn in two by her conflicting interests.

During the war of the League of Augsburg, commercial connection between England and France was entirely prohibited. The Scots Parliament and Privy Council occasionally issued Acts and Proclamations against commerce and correspondence with France, but it does not appear that any of the authorities really tried to enforce the prohibitions. Various cases of their infringe-

---

[1] *S. P. C. R.*, 10 Sept. 1663.

ment are mentioned in the Privy Council Register, but always in the form of a complaint by merchants that English privateers had illegally taken it upon themselves to examine Scots ships—a complaint endorsed by the Council. France, during the war, imposed new duties on some imports, including the chief articles of Scottish trade. In 1697 the Convention of the Royal Burghs represented to the Privy Council " what discouradgements the trade and commerce of this kingdome is under through the heavie impositiones and burdenes that are upon the goodes they import to France, as particularly ther Scots woollens, butter, linnen cloath, coalls and all other goods imported to France....As also the fishing of this natione, which is undenyably the farr greatest manufactury thereof cannot be vended in France, being under an absolute prohibitione only since the beginning of the lait warr[1]." The Scots were anxious to be represented in the " treaty of commerce to be held betwix your subjects of Brittane and those of France," in order that " the matter of trade may be adjusted and your subjects of this kingdome restored to their antient priuieledges[2]." But no concessions were made to Scotland when the Peace of Ryswick was concluded in 1697, which was a cause of much complaint. Fletcher of Saltoun declared that in this affair the Scottish nation would have been well advised had they supported a minister of their own, "who might have obtained the reestablishment of the Nation in the Priviledges they had in France, which was totally neglected : And notwithstanding the great and unproportionable numbers of Sea and Land Soldiers that we were

[1] *Royal Burghs*, IV., p. 259.   [2] *Ibid.*, p. 248.

obliged to furnish for the support of the war, yet not one tittle of advantage was procured to us by the Peace[1]."

As it was evident that nothing could be done to restore the Scottish privileges in France by English negotiation, the Scots began to urge the adoption of retaliatory measures. The Committee of Trade resolved "that ye tread with ffrance is most prejudiciall to this nations interest in respect that they have annulled the priviledges of ye Scots nation in ffrance and of late have prohibited the import of Scots goods by Scots men...by impositions equivalent to ane prohibitione and as a remedy it is proposed that ye import of ffrench goods be discharged untill ye Scots priviledges be restored and those incumbrances and heavy impositions be taken off[2]." Accordingly in 1701 the "Act Dischargeing Wine Brandie and all other Liquors of the grouth of France" was passed[3]. It provided that "this prohibition shall continue ay and while the same liberties and immunities be granted to herrings and all other goods imported from this Kingdom into France and the same freedom and immunities granted to Scots ships sailing thither that any other Nation enjoy in that Kingdom." With this Act as a basis for negotiation the Scots endeavoured to treat with France on their own account. In August of the same year, Mr Alexander Cunninghame wrote from Paris to Carstares that he had at last succeeded in interviewing Count de Torcy about Scottish trade. "He asked to see a power from the King of England and would give no answer to the removing their edict till the King of England did give me authority

[1] Fletcher, *Second Discourse*, p. 16.
[2] *Parliamentary Papers*, xv., 86.
[3] *Acts, Scotland*, x., p. 278.

to treat...if the King of England would appoint Commissioners presently, that the treaty might be concluded very soon...and that the French King would be easily disposed to grant to the Scottish nation their antient privileges or other new ones that would be more for the benefit of commerce[1]." But the King of England would give no authority, and these negotiations were fruitless. Indeed in 1701 greater impositions were laid upon goods "du crû et fabrique d'Angleterre, Écosse, Irlande et pays en dépendant[2]." The prohibition did not entirely put a stop to the trade with France. The tacksmen of the customs demanded, and received, a reduction in the tack because of their loss through the prohibition of the import of French wines. It was, however, pointed out that "even the prohibitions were not so strictly observed but that the tacksmen had full benefit by import of the very goods prohibited[3]." The prohibition policy, however, was not successful. There must have been considerable decrease in the trade, for the customs decreased, and the custom on French wines had been the chief fund for the civil list. Also the French trade was very important to the country. Unless an Act allowing the trade again were passed, it was said "the subjects may plow up their towns and burn their ships[4]." Accordingly in 1703 the Scottish Parliament passed the "Act allowing the Importation of Wines and other Forreign Liquors," and also the "Act anent Peace and Warr[5]," which made a great stir in both

---

[1] *Carstares Papers*, p. 709.

[2] P. Clément, *Histoire du Système Protecteur en France*, p. 283.

[3] *Customs and Foreign Excise, Miscellaneous Papers*, 1692–1707.

[4] *The Proceedings of the Parliament of Scotland. Begun at Edinburgh, 6th May*, 1703. Advocates' Library, Pamphlets, Vol. 89.

[5] *Acts, Scotland*, xi., pp. 107, 112.

countries. The two Acts were generally considered to hang together. " The Scots Wine Act makes a great noise in this place. I have heard some members of Parliament declare they look upon it as the opening a back door to the enemies of England, and as putting in practice already their other Act whereby they are empowered to observe a neutrality in the wars of England when they please[1]." Burnet's account of the matter is as follows: " Another act of a strange nature passed, allowing the imposition of French goods...The truth was, the revenue was so exhausted that they had not enough to support the government without such help: those who desired to drink good wine, and all who were concerned in trade, ran into it, so it was carried, tho' with great opposition. The Jacobites also went into it, since it opened a free correspondence with France; it was certainly against the public interest of the government[2]." The " Wine Act" was the last contribution of the legislature to Scotland's struggle for trade with France, so we may now turn to examine the amount and the nature of the trade actually carried on during the time when trade between England and France was prohibited.

In 1691 the captain of the ship *Pembroke*, sent by the Lords of the Admiralty to examine boats suspected of trading with France, wrote from Greenock: " In my last I gave you an account that the Scots had a free trade with France, which I now confirm....I heard of one Francis Duncombe, master of the John, pink, whom I followed to this place, intending to have examined him, but above

[1] *Letter to Harley, from London, H. M. C. R., Portland Papers*, IV., p. 70.

[2] Burnet, *History of his own Times*, v., p. 95.

20 of his men presented their arms at me,...and farther
they told me that free trading was allowed in these parts
with France, and their merchants must live[1]." Later
Mr Trumbull wrote to Mr Secretary Johnstone upon a
matter, which, he said, the Lords Justices preferred to
refer to the Lords of the Admiralty instead of directly to
His Majesty, namely, "a Complaint of a Trade driven
with ffrance by some of Scotland...this unlawfull Practice
so very prejudiciall to his Ma^{ty}[2]." Although corn was not
one of the chief exports to France, there were several
complaints from England during the wars that corn from
Scotland supplied the enemy with victual. In 1694 the
Queen wrote to the Scottish Privy Council complaining of
the export of corn to France to "supply the necessities of
our enemies." The Privy Council answered that corn had
not been sent there; "But to our Regrate The Supply of
Cornes that our Enemies have had from us Hath been by
their Privateers taking our ships all allongst our coasts."
In spite of the denial of the Privy Council it seems, from
other complaints, that the Queen had some ground for
her remonstrance. A considerable number of Scottish
merchants settled in Dublin, whence they carried provisions, both Irish and Scottish, and information, to France.
Mr Francis Babe, an official in Dublin, says that "there
was a Trade frequently carried on by Scotch Merchants
that resides in this Citty...between ffrance and Ireland,
by reason of which trade, the enemy were supplied with
great Quantities of our provisions, and especially in the
year 1693 when the Commonality of ffrance were perishing

---

[1] *S. P. Domestic, William III, Home Office, Admiralty*, IV., p. 101.
[2] *Ibid., Letter Book (Secretary's)*, III., p. 195 (1695).

for want of bread, that intelligence by letters were sent
from this Citty to Rochell, that gave Account of our
Navall preparations for making a descent into ffrance, and
that in short time after sending that intelligence we were
unsuccessful in our attempt on St Mallo[1]." Many complaints were made about the transport of English wool
from Scotland to France, where it was used in the French
cloth manufacture[2].

The English also complained of the import into England of prohibited French goods from Scotland. In 1705
the Privy Council wrote to the Lord Lieutenant of
Cumberland, that Her Majesty in Council had "received
information of an evil practice of bringing tobacco, brandy
and other commodities into this Kingdom out of Scotland
by land, without paying the usual duties according to
law." Also when seizures had been made by the officers
"the said commodities have been rescued from them by
numbers of men assembled together in a tumultuous
manner, armed with clubs, plough coulters and other
instruments of iron[3]."

Endeavours were made by the English government to
stop this trade with France. English privateers and men-
of-war cruised about the Scottish coasts in order to arrest
ships suspected of trading with France or the Plantations.
This interference was resented by the merchants, and also
by the Privy Council, on the grounds of damage to their
trade, and that, "as Scotland is ane absolute kingdome
soe neither England nor other fforaigners Have the Least
power within the Scotts waters and harbours And that

---

[1] *Treasury Papers*, xxxv., 27.
[2] See above, pp. 103—109.
[3] *H. M. C. R.*, App. VI., MSS. of the Earl of Carlisle, p. 11.

any Attempts made by them of this Kynde Is ane Hayle
Violatione of the Law of Nationes[1]." In 1694 the Glasgow
merchants declared that a small ship cruised in the Clyde,
and "under a pretence of a Commissione from the Admiralty of England for Searching after goods from ffrance
or from America Enters aboard all Shipps Coming out from
or Going Into Clyde and takes provisions and what else
He finds." The merchants suggested that a "shipp of
fforce" should be equipped, and sent out to apprehend
such vessels, and to "secure the River of Clyde from all
such who may disturbe their trade[2]." They offered to
provide and equip the ship if the government would send
seamen. In the same year the Privy Council wrote to
the King, that trade was so much interrupted by the
interference of English ships that "our merchants are soe
much discouradged and prejudged...that many of them
already hes given over trade and the rest must follow
their example[3]." Some years later the merchants of
Edinburgh, on behalf of themselves and the other merchants of the kingdom, complained that "we are wholly
frustrat of our Trade to Portugal Lighurn or any other
free port in the Streights, for the English do carry up all
ships belonging to Scotland for any of these Places...
suspecting that our ships are going to France[4]." After
the passing of the "Wine Act," the English became still
more alarmed about Scottish correspondence with France.
In September, 1704, Roxburgh wrote from London that
the House of Lords were about to address the Queen,

[1] *S. P. C. R.*, 22 May 1693.

[2] *Ibid.*, 27 Sept. 1694.

[3] *Ibid.*, 29 June 1694.

[4] *Parliamentary Papers*, xxi., 190.

"to have ships sett in such and such stations for taking of Scotch ships going or coming from France[1]."

Scottish trade did not only suffer from English ships attacking her vessels because of their trade with France, but also from French attacks because of her connection with England. She was thus doubly handicapped throughout the war. All the time the tacksmen of the customs received many complaints from merchants whose ships had been seized by the French, and also claims for the remission of duty or for compensation. Some of these were granted. The tacksmen for the years 1691 to 1696 allowed £2901. 7s. 5d. to several merchants as "abatements for duty upon ships taken during the French war[2]." One Glasgow merchant and his partners lost twenty-two ships and their cargoes between 1690 and 1698, and two more in 1699 and 1700, one "loaded with linnings, herrings etc bound for Madera and the other homeward bound from Norway[3]."

Altogether the Scots merchants suffered very much from these wars. They attributed their losses largely to their union with England. "We come next to propose the state of our Trade with France. The loss of our Ancient Alliance with that Famous and Great Kingdom and of the Honourable and Advantagious Priviledges we enjoyed there is one of the great Damages we sustain'd by the Union of the Crowns[4]." Another writer summed up the situation very well. "Seeing most of the Trade of Scotland lieth with neighbouring Nations and especially

---

[1] *Jerviswood Correspondence* (Bannatyne Club), p. 21.
[2] *Customs and Foreign Excise, Tacksmen's Accompts,* Vol. VII.
[3] *Acts, Scotland,* XI., p. 49.
[4] *Scotland's Grievances Relating to Darien etc.,* Part II., p. 29.

those which England hath oftnest provocation to quarrel with, and the Scots driving very little Traffick with Countries far remote; it consequently follows that upon the Commencement of a War with those adjacent States and Kingdoms the Scots do become in a manner shut out from, and deprived of all foreign Trade; while in the meantime the English do continue to carry on a vast and Beneficiall Trade to Turkey Affrik and the East Indies, as well as to and from their own American Plantations." These considerations, amongst others, convinced Scotland of the necessity of making some change in her relationship towards England, and Scotland's determination to continue her French connection did much to bring the English to the same conclusions.

g. Trade with Holland, etc.

Scottish trade with Holland also suffered through England's wars. This was very disastrous, as a great part of her commerce was with Dutch ports. Charles II's Dutch wars lasted from 1665 to 1674, with a few short intervals, ten years which brought Scotland's trade and finances to a very low ebb. The commercial community had not had time to recover from the effects of the Civil Wars, and this war, their "greatest and readiest trading being with Holland," still further reduced their resources. Poverty was so great that it was difficult to raise men and supplies for England's war, in which, as the Scots said, "our hazard is greater, and I am sure they intend us noe profit how successful soever the war be[1]." As time went on, it became more and more difficult to raise any money

[1] Tweeddale to Lauderdale, *Lauderdale Papers*, i., p. 213.

for this purpose. The revenue was much reduced by the want of trade caused by the war. The Commissioners of the Treasury wrote in 1672 that the revenue had been reduced by a third in the last war with Holland, and that they expected about the same decrease during the present war[1]. The customs receipts were in fact reduced from £17,362. 10s. in 1665 to £6,481. 13s. 4d. in 1666, but during the war of 1672–74 they did not fall so low. "We are," writes Rothes in 1665, "like as we were besieged, for in no place in the whole world have we any commerce at this time, and money does grow daily scarcer so as in a short time there will I believe be none[2]." The discontent was so great that a rebellion in connection with a Dutch invasion was feared. "The least commotion in England or Ireland or encouragement from foreigners abroad would certainly engage us in a new rebellion[3]." At the beginning of the second war, it was given out in London that the Scots had offered to continue trade with the Dutch, and to shelter their ships in Scottish harbours in spite of the war with England[4]. This was probably a figment of English imagination, but it testifies to the ever existent English jealousy of the Scottish connection with Holland. As a matter of fact, there was very little trade with the Dutch during the war, far less than there was with France during the later French wars.

After the Treaty of Breda in 1667, the Scots staple port was moved from Campvere to Dort[5]. It was said that this step was taken at the instigation of the De Witts.

[1] *Lauderdale Papers*, ii., p. 222.　　[2] *Ibid.*, i., p. 220.
[3] Burnet to Sheldon, *Lauderdale Papers*, i., p. 215, n.
[4] *S. P. Domestic, Charles II*, cccvii., 190.
[5] *Historical Account of the Scots Staple Port.*

They wished the prosperity which the Scottish trade brought to come to Dort, which was under their influence, rather than to Campvere where the Orange faction was supreme. This was an unfortunate step for Scottish trade. Dort was not so conveniently situated for their ships, and so, though some merchants settled there, others remained at Campvere, and some went to Amsterdam and Rotterdam. Although the staple was again fixed at Campvere in 1676[1], it was never afterwards the same resort of Scots trade and merchants as it had been before the war. They now congregated more at Rotterdam, which was not only a far more important commercial centre than Campvere, but was also a favourite refuge for those Presbyterians who left the country on account of the Stewarts' ecclesiastical policy. Rotterdam and Dort were each anxious that an arrangement should be made with them about the import of Scots coal, which was not then a staple commodity[2]. At Rotterdam Scottish coal entered into competition with English. The magistrates were anxious to come to some agreement with the Scots because of " the small export they " (the English) " mak in respect of the Scottishe Natione[3]." The Scots coal trade seems to have flourished, for in 1684 complaints were made to the Customs Commissioners in England that France, Holland, and other foreign markets were " extraordinarily supplied with Coales from Scotland in Strangers Ships to the great prejudice of the English Navigation and damnage to his Majesty's customs here[4]."

S. P. C. R., 5 Sept. 1676.   [2] Scottish Staple at Veere, p. 225.

[3] British Museum, Maitland and Lauderdale MSS. 35,125, f. 210.

[4] British Museum, Add. MSS. 28079. Mr Ettrick's paper about exported coales, 20 Dec. 1684.

Altogether the trade between Scotland and Holland was considerable. Josiah Child declared that "The Trades of Scotland and Ireland, two of our own Kingdoms, the Dutch have bereaved us of, and in effect wholly Engrossed to themselves[1]."

The principal goods which the Scots took to Holland were plaiding and fingrains, wool, skins, hides, stockings, salmon, butter, tallow, beef, coals, etc. Scots ships also imported to Holland wine and salt from the south, and corn from the Baltic and "Easter Seas[2]." From the Dutch the Scots received chiefly all sorts of manufactured goods, some of which they had doubtless brought from England before the English Navigation Acts had forced them to retaliate by putting high duties on English imports. After the Dutch wars the country was too poor to employ all the shipping, and so the "Ships of this Kingdom wer for the most part ffraughted by Hollanders who gave them greater ffraughts than Scots merchds Which made a considerable interruption of tred in this Kingdom[3]." Later in the century, when Scottish trade recovered, Scottish merchants had not enough ships for their own use, and so employed a number of Dutch ships. In 1697 the contract with Campvere was again renewed for twenty-one years[4], but after the Union, when the export of wool and skins, the principal articles of Scots trade, was forbidden, the trade decreased very much.

The Scots trade with the "Easter Seas" and the Baltic

[1] *New Discourse of Trade*, Josiah Child.

[2] *Royal Burghs*, III., p. 671.

[3] Petition of Tacksmen of the Excise for Abatement, 1677. *Customs, Miscellaneous Papers*, 1597–1692.

[4] *Royal Burghs*, IV., p. 217.

increased during the French wars, as it was safer from
French attacks than the Low Countries trade. In Stockholm there were, in 1660, twelve Scottish ship captains
settled, as compared with twenty of Lübeck, and twenty-
eight of Holland[1]. A number of Scots ships also traded
with Norway, bringing home chiefly timber, and taking
out woollen manufactures and "victuall." In 1680 the
Burghs complained of the "great impositions imposed by
the King of Denmark upon Scots victuall...at the seuerall
ports in Norraway and other ports within the said King's
dominions[2]." Some merchants even penetrated as far as
Archangel.

In Königsberg there was a struggle between the
magistrates and the Scots, whose success in business had
aroused jealousy against them. New taxes were imposed
on them, and there seems to have been some threat to
expel them altogether. The Churfürst, however, was
strongly in their favour, and owing to his influence, the
magistrates desisted from their opposition to the Scots[3].
A few years later the Scots at Königsberg obtained permission to build a church for themselves there, for which
collections were authorised in Scotland in 1697[4] and
1699[5]. The masters of Scots ships at Dantzig in 1706
appealed for convoys for twenty-five or thirty ships which
were to sail for Scotland in the summer[6]

At Hamburg the Scots had some trouble because of
the exclusive privileges of the English merchants who
traded there. The Scots were said to be debarred from

---

[1] *Scots in Sweden*, p. 41.　　　　[2] *Royal Burghs*, III., p. 23.
[3] *Scots in East and West Prussia*, Tho. A. Fischer, pp. 71—73.
[4] *S. P. C. R.*, 7 Apr. 1697.　　　　[5] *Royal Burghs*, IV., p. 231.
[6] *H. M. C. R.*, *Mar and Kellie Papers*, p. 262.

trade, as subjects of the King of England who were not members of the English company. They declared that they were subjects of Scotland, not England, and were " as free to trade there as any other nation," and requested that the English staple might be " discharged to truble any Scotts merchand tradeing there[1]." They were not, after this, prevented from trading, but the illogical nature of the position is evident. In the Plantation trade the Scots were not considered English subjects, as it was not to England's advantage that they should have freedom of trade there. Where it would be possible to take dues from them as English subjects, they were placed in that category. The Scots themselves, as illogical as the English, sought or evaded the name as best suited their own convenience and profit.

In the Mediterranean, orders were given that the Scots should share the privileges by passports, etc., which were secured by treaty to the subjects of the King of Great Britain, from the governments of Algiers, Tripoli and Tunis[2]. Some guarantee or defence was very necessary against the pirates of those parts, who were very active, not only in the Mediterranean, but on the coasts of France and Spain. Many Scottish ships trading to Portugal, the Bay of Biscay ports, and Cadiz, were taken, and petitions for collections to be made in the churches to ransom captives among the Turks were very numerous.

The dangers to trade from men-of-war, privateers, and pirates were great ; and also from the state of the coast, unguarded by lighthouses and buoys, and not even properly described in charts or maps. In 1695, an attempt was made to organise a survey of the whole coast

[1] *Royal Burghs*, IV., pp. 41, 28.

[2] *H.M.C.R.,Buccleugh and Queensferry Papers*, Vol. II., Part I. p. 181.

of Scotland. To defray the expenses, an imposition of
10*s.* per ton was imposed on all foreign vessels trading
with Scotland, and of 4*s.* per ton on all Scots shipping.
The duty caused many complaints. The shipowners
grumbled because of the duty on Scots ships, which were
thus put at a disadvantage in their foreign trade, as they
had already to pay duties in foreign ports. The coalowners complained that the duty was so high that foreign
ships did not come for coals, but went to Newcastle
instead[1]. The imposition was not removed, but in 1698
the duty on foreign ships was reduced to 8*s.* on those exporting coal, and raised to 24*s.* on all others. The 4*s.*
duty on native ships, except on those of the African
Company, was continued for five years[2]. The proceeds
were used to maintain frigates for the defence of the coast
as well as for the survey.

On the whole, Scottish trade suffered from the English
connection. The Scots had to contribute men and money
to wars which interrupted their trade, and from which
they reaped no advantages in the end. England had practically no control over Scottish trade, and was jealous of
her connection with France and Holland, and indeed of
any trade in which Scottish interests came into competition with those of England. Abroad, the Scottish
merchants were in an ambiguous position. They did not
wish to come under the authority of the English representatives, even when they had no representatives of their
own, and in cases where there was a Scots agent, he often
came into conflict with the English influences and
interests. Altogether neither party found the state of
affairs at all satisfactory.

[1] *Parliamentary Papers*, xv., 16 ; xvi., 16.
[2] *Acts, Scotland*, x., p. 175.

CHAPTER V

THE COMPANY OF SCOTLAND TRADING TO AFRICA AND THE INDIES

SCOTLAND'S illicit trade with the Plantations did not compensate for the drawbacks to her European trade caused by William's wars, and to her English trade by high duties on her imports. Her industries had developed, and their production was increasing, so she felt more and more keenly the want of markets for her goods. The Scots regretted and bemoaned their poverty, and began to realise that "this Nation, of all those who possess good Ports, and lie conveniently for Trade and Fishing, has bin the only part of Europe which did not apply itself to Commerce." Therefore, according to Fletcher of Saltoun, "by an unforeseen and unexpected change of the genius of this nation all their thoughts and inclinations...seem to be turned upon Trade[1]." It was obvious that a colonial market of their own was what the Scots really needed. The promoters of the New Jersey colony had pointed out that their settlement would prove of great advantage to the country, as increasing the consumption of Scottish manufactures. A few years later (1691) the Commissioners

[1] Fletcher, *First Discourse concerning the affairs of Scotland.*

for the burgh of Glasgow declared "that it is the great concern of the royall borrows to have ane interest in forraigne plantations," and suggested that settlements might be made in Carolina and the West Indian Islands. The Convention considered the matter, but at that time nothing came of it[1]. In 1693 the question of foreign plantations was brought before the Committee of Trade[2], and in the same year was passed the "Act for Encouraging of Forraigne Trade[3]." This Act offered to all companies which should be formed for carrying on foreign trade, all the privileges and immunities which were granted to manufacturing companies. These were to be confirmed by Letters Patent from the King, and further, if attacks were made on the property of such companies, restitution was to be enforced "by publick means and at publick expense." These privileges were more comprehensive than those enjoyed by any English company, and they were also to receive confirmation from Parliament.

The English commercial community was at this time, and had been for some years, much agitated by a controversy which raged round the East India trade. After the Restoration, when the charter granted by Cromwell in 1657 was renewed, this trade had flourished greatly, and those concerned in it became extremely wealthy. But the profits were confined to comparatively few, and the management of the company was entirely in their hands. It was, in fact, a very close monopoly. The possibility of such great gain induced private traders to fit out and send ships to the East, and gradually these interlopers, as they

---

[1] *Royal Burghs*, IV., p. 133.

[2] *Parliamentary Papers*, XIV., 99.

[3] *Acts, Scotland*, IX., p. 314

were called, became quite a numerous body. They were
engaged in a continual struggle with the company, who
were determined to maintain their monopoly. Sir Josiah
Child, a "commercial grandee, who in wealth and the
influence that attends wealth, vied with the greatest
nobles of his time," governor of the company, was the
leader in the contest with the interlopers. By costly
presents and judicious bribes he made a place for himself
high in Court favour, and secured from James II a charter
maintaining the monopoly.   Just after this, a quarrel
between the Mogul government and the company agents
led to war in India.   While this was going on, the Revolution deprived Sir Josiah of Court support, and made
an opportunity for his opponents, of which they were not
slow to avail themselves. They were for the most part
anxious rather for the formation of a company which
should be governed neither by a despot nor by an oli-
garchy, than for an entirely unregulated trade.   These
persons formed themselves into a society known as the
New Company, which now carried on the struggle against
the Old, Child's, Company.   Both were most anxious to
obtain parliamentary powers, but though the latter
secured a renewal of its privileges by charter in 1693,
authority from Parliament was still denied.

After the charter was obtained, the company dealt
very harshly with the interlopers, and the question was
in consequence referred to the consideration of the House
of Commons. The result was that, in 1694, the Commons
passed a resolution declaring "that it was the right of all
Englishmen to trade to the East Indies or any part of the
world, unless prohibited by Act of Parliament."   Trade,
though nominally free, was still largely controlled by the

Old Company, who had factories and offices in India. The New Company, in spite of their efforts, were not able to procure a charter. The position of affairs in 1695, therefore, was that in England there were many merchants most anxious to obtain parliamentary privileges for their trade, and that in Scotland extensive parliamentary privileges were offered, and there were few merchants who had sufficient capital or knowledge to take advantage of them.

The idea of combining the two, with great advantage to Scotland, was conceived by a certain William Paterson. He was a man of considerable commercial and financial genius. He had drawn up a scheme for a national bank, which was accepted by the English Parliament in 1694, and for a short time he was a director of the thus formed Bank of England. He had travelled a good deal, especially in the West Indies, and from his knowledge of those regions sprang his scheme for an international *entrepôt* on the Panama Isthmus. He is said to have tried to push this scheme in some continental trading centres, without success. Then he came to London, but there seems to have contented himself with suggestions for carrying on the East India trade, under cover of an Act to be secured from the Scottish Parliament. Doubtless he intended, when the company was formed, to bring forward his plan of trading to the East Indies *viâ* the Isthmus and the Pacific, but this was kept in the background for the present. Some English merchants took up the scheme warmly. Then the projectors went to Scotland, where, as has been pointed out, the nation was anxious to establish some new trade connections. The instructions given to Tweeddale, Lord High Commissioner, for the current session of Parliament, included directions to pass an Act "for the encouragement of such as shall acquire and establish a plantation in Africa or America or in any other part of the world where plantations may be lawfully acquired," with "such rights and privileges as we grant in like case to the subjects of our other dominions the one not interfering with the other[1]." These instructions were given in April.

Early in May, according to Paterson, a London merchant informed him that there was "great Encouragement given for an East Indian Company in Scotland; upon which he" (i.e. Paterson) "gave Mr Chiesly a Scheme for creating the same; but that was not entirely followed[2]." Perhaps Paterson's original plan laid some stress on his Panama scheme. Two merchants then proceeded to Scotland, and in June 1693, the "Act for a Company Tradeing to Affrica and the Indies[3]" was passed. Twenty-one persons, some of whom were English, were constituted a corporation, receiving certain great privileges. They were empowered to trade with Asia, Africa, and America; to plant colonies in places not already possessed by any European power; to defend their trade and colonies "by force of Arms"; to make reprisals for any damage done them; to conclude treaties with foreign powers; and to have all rights of government and admiralty in their colonies. All their ships and goods were to be free from customs and duties for twenty-one years. The Scots Navigation Act of 1661 was suspended in their favour, and they were granted a monopoly of trade to Africa, America, and the Indies, "excepting and without any

---

[1] S. P. Domestic, Scotland, Warrant Book, xvi., 11.
[2] Paterson's Evidence, Commons Journals, xi., p. 400.
[3] Acts, Scotland, ix., p. 377.

prejudice to any of the Subjects of this Kingdom to trade
and navigat...to any part of America where the Collonies
plantations or possessions of the said Company shall not
be setled," that is, of course, reserving the Scots trade to
the English Plantations. Lastly, His Majesty promised to
interpose his authority to have restitution made for any
harm done to the company. This Act was clearly the
work of an independent Scots Parliament. In pre-
Revolution days, when Court influence was supreme,
through the Lords of the Articles, such an Act could not
have been passed. The official who now represented the
Court, Tweeddale, Lord High Commissioner, obviously
went beyond his instructions. Burnet says that the King
" drew an instruction impowering the commissioner to pass
a bill promising letters patent for encouraging of trade,
yet limited, so that it should not interfere with the
trade of England : when they went down to Scotland, the
king's commissioner either did not consider this, or had
no regard to it; for he gave the royal assent to an act,
that gave the undertakers either of the East India or
West India trade, all possible privileges[1]." The King's
answer to the English Parliament's address on the subject:
" I have been ill Served in Scotland," is well known.
Tweeddale was dismissed from office for this piece of
work.

The Act required that half the capital should be
raised in Scotland, and amongst the promoters there were
ten Scotsmen. The English merchants, however, were
really the moving influence of the concern, and accordingly
the first attempts to float the company were made in

[1] *History of his own Times*, Burnet, IV., p. 277.

London. The probability of jealousy and interference on the part of the English Parliament and merchants was recognised from the first. Paterson wrote on 9 July from London (the Act was passed on 26 June): "the Gentlemen here...thinke also that we ought to keep private and close for some months that no occasion may be given for the Parliament of England directly or indirectly to take notice of it in the ensueing Session, which might be of ill consequence and especially since a great many considerable persons are already allarum'd at it." Paterson seems to have realised distinctly at this time that Scotland could not hope to carry out the scheme alone: "We must engage some of the best heads and purses for Trade in Europe therein, or we can never do it as it ought to be." Unfortunately, neither the "best heads" nor the "best purses" had any share in the undertaking in its final form. Paterson's prophecy, written at the same time, was unfortunately fulfilled: "we may be sure, should we only Settle some little Colony or Plantation and send some ships They would looke upon them as Interlopers and all agree to discourage and crush us to pieces[1]."

The meetings of those concerned in the company were held in London, beginning on 29 August 1695. At first only the English promoters were present, and the meetings were called meetings "of Gentlemen concerned in the Company of Scotland trading to Africa and the Indies." The dilatoriness of the Scottish members in coming to London, or even in writing, was at first a great source of trouble to the English undertakers. Paterson wrote repeatedly urging them to hasten, but they did not arrive

---

[1] *Darien Papers* (Bannatyne Club), p. 2.

until 9 November. Henceforward the meetings were styled "Meeting of the Company of Scotland trading to Affrica and the Indies." The subscription books were opened on 6 November, and the company met with so much encouragement that the capital, originally fixed at £360,000, was raised to £600,000, of which the £300,000 to be raised in England was speedily subscribed. The sum paid up was £75,000. There was much anxiety that the books should be closed before the opening of Parliament, and this was done on the same day, 22 November, that the session of Parliament began. The English East India Company had already (11 November) taken notice of the Scots company, by voting that any of its members who were concerned in the Scots company would break their oath to the English company. They also petitioned the King for assistance.

On 2 December, the Lords resolved to consider the Scots Act. Next day they ordered the merchants trading to the East and West Indies, and the Customs Commissioners to attend the House, "to give an Account wherein the Act of Parliament lately made in Scotland for a Company trading to Africa and the Indies may be prejudicial to the Trade of this Kingdom into those parts[1]." They appeared next day, and pointed out the extent of the Scots privileges, their exemption from customs and other duties, the exclusion of interlopers, and also their power of making reprisals. On the 4th the directors of the company met, and resolved that "one or more Ship or Ships be fitted out for the East Indies from Scotland with all convenient speed[2]." Their last meeting was on 7 December,

---

[1] *Lords Journals*, xv., p. 603.
[2] *Commons Journals*, xi., p. 405.

and on the same day the subscription books of the company were ordered to be laid before the House of Lords,
and some of the directors were ordered to appear before
the House[1]. On the 13th the Lords agreed to an address
on the subject of the Scots company to be presented to
the King, in which the Commons concurred. In this it
was pointed out that the company's freedom from all
duties and customs would make Scotland the staple for
Indian and colonial goods, and that thereby England's
trade would be ruined. Also that his Majesty's promise to
enforce restitution for any damage done to the company's
possessions "does seem to engage Your Majesty to employ
the Shipping and Strength at Sea of this Nation, to
support this new Company to the great Detriment even
of this Kingdom[2]." In the MSS. minutes of the House
of Lords for the same day, this entry stands: "Moved
that a day may be appointed to receive what may be
proposed in order to have union between England and
Scotland[3]." Even in the very heat of the controversy, it
was realised by some that a union was the only means by
which the interests of the countries could be made identical, and the dangers from an independent Scots Parliament obviated. A few days later it was suggested that
certain bills should be prepared, dealing with the different
points brought up in the address. The first was to
discourage all Englishmen " under severe Penalties from
engaging in the Stock and Management of the Scots East
India Company"; and another was to prohibit English
seamen from serving the Scots company, and English

---

[1] *Lords Journals*, xv., p. 608.   [2] *Ibid.*, p. 611.
[3] For the History of the Company in England see articles by Hiram
Bingham in the *Scottish Historical Review*, 1906, pp. 210, 316, 637.

shipbuilders from building for them[1]. The Lords now dropped the matter, but in January it was taken up again by the Commons. The East India Company complained that those concerned in the Scots company were fitting out ships for the Indies, and the House ordered an inquiry to be made into all the circumstances of the founding of the company[2]. Accordingly, on 21 January 1696, the secretary and several of the directors were examined. The books had been sent off to Scotland, and therefore could not be brought before the House. One director said he had "resolved to act no longer," when he heard that Parliament had taken up the matter. Another, a member of the English East India Company, subscribed £3000, but when he heard it was resolved to send out a ship, he refused, saying: "It was against his Oath to the English East India Company. And further That if the Ship was lost, the Scotts might refuse to bear their Parts." On the same day it was resolved to impeach all the directors[3]. Nothing came of this resolution, but parliamentary inquiry was fatal to the interests of the company, and almost all the English subscribers withdrew.

In agitating against the Scottish company, the great English companies had a twofold object in view. No doubt they were honestly alarmed at the prospect of a company with such extensive privileges, largely financed and managed by Englishmen, making Scotland an emporium, and greatly damaging their trade. But in addition, both the East India and African companies intended to make capital out of the general alarm. The East India Company seized the opportunity of pointing out that their

---

[1] *Lords Journals*, xv., p. 618.
[2] *Commons Journals*, xi., p. 398.   [3] *Ibid.*, pp. 401, 407.

trade was "in Danger of being lost, by means of the great Privileges granted to Joint Stocks of neighbouring Nations," and praying for leave to bring in a bill to establish their company[1]. The Lords suggested on 20 December, that bills should be prepared to establish the East India and Africa Companies in England, "with such Powers and Privileges as shall be proper to obviate the Inconveniences that may otherwise arise by the Scotch Act[2]." But excitement over the Scots Act soon died down, and the Company was not successful in its attempt to obtain parliamentary authority. On the other hand, those who were anxious that the trade should be open to all, drew another moral from the Scots Act. "And if all Englishmen have the freedom of trade to India it cannot be supposed any of them will joyn with the Scotch, but everyone will rather imploy his own money." This, the writer declared, would ruin the Scots company. "Now if all the English decline the Scots Company, they will want both Stock and Experience to carry it on, and will sink of themselves"—a true prophecy.

The matter was also considered in relation to the Plantation trade. Randolph, government agent in the Colonies, wrote soon after the Act was passed, that the Scots, "under pretence of Erecting an East India Company in y[t] Kingdome...do Engage themselves with Great Sums of money in an American Trade; a Trade which has already for Several Years been carried on by Scotchmen." He feared that they might make a settlement in some unappropriated spot near Pennsylvania, or in an island near the coast, which might become "a staple not only of all Sorts

[1] *Commons Journals*, xi., p. 365.
[2] *Lords Journals*, xv., p. 618.

of European Manufactures, but also of the Enumerated Plantation Commodities[1]." Like the East India Company, Randolph used the Scots project as a stalking horse for impressing on the government the necessity for those measures which he desired, the tightening up and stricter enforcement of the Navigation Acts, and the necessity of joining small proprietary colonies to the government of some province directly under His Majesty's authority. The Lords, influenced by the Customs Commissioners, also paid some attention to this aspect of the Scots Act. They ordered the Commissioners to attend the House, "to give an Account, whether as the Law now stands, there be a sufficient Power, in Carolina, Maryland, Pennsilvania and other Plantations where there are Proprietors to collect the King's Duties there : and whether there be the same Security to prevent the Inconveniences that may arise to the Proprietors and Planters there, from the Act of Parliament in Scotland[2]." These inquiries were followed by the "Act for preventing Frauds and Regulating Abuses in the Plantation Trade[3]." Besides making the regulations more stringent, with a view to checking the existing Scottish trade, the Act took some precautions against a Scottish settlement being founded, by declaring that no land in the colonies was to be sold to any but natives of England, Ireland, or the Plantations. The agitators against the Scots Act connected with the Plantation trade were therefore more successful than the traders to the East. Parliament considered the Plantation trade of greater importance to England than the Indian trade, as in America there was a better market for

[1] *S. P. Col., Col. Entry Book*, c., 352.
[2] *Lords Journals*, xv., p. 619.   [3] 7 & 8 Gul. III, c. 22.

England's chief product, woollen cloth; and also the returns
from the colonies were esteemed of more value than the
goods which were brought from the East. They were
therefore anxious both to stop the Scottish trade with the
West, which already went on, and also to prevent the
Scots from securing any land near the colonies, where
they might establish a depôt for colonial goods, and from
which, with the help of Dutch shipping, Europe might be
supplied.

English opposition and parliamentary investigation
converted the company from a possible success into a
probable failure. The promoters were now dependent on
Scottish support. This was most ungrudgingly given, all
the more because Scottish national pride was aroused by
English interference. " Scots humours seem no less warm
in prosecuting this business than the Inglish are in
opposing it....T'was the notice the parliament of Ingland
first took of it made the wholl nation throng in to have
some share and I'm of opinion the resentments people are
acted by; are the greatest supplys (that) furnishes life to
that affaire[1]." The books were opened in Edinburgh on
26 February 1696. Over £50,000 was subscribed on the
first day, and by the end of July the whole amount, fixed
now at £400,000 instead of £300,000, was subscribed.
The largest subscribers were the Duke of Hamilton,
Lord Belhaven and Stewart of Grandtully, who each
subscribed £3000. Landed proprietors, merchants, ship-
owners and masters, manufacturers, advocates, writers,
doctors, craftsmen, all invested, the sums varying from
£2000 to £100.

[1] *H. M. C. R.*, xii., Part VIII., p. 58.   Cockburn, Lord Justice Clerk,
to Lord Tullibardine (Dec. 1697).

But as the capital had been originally fixed at £600,000, it was felt that efforts should be made to raise the additional £200,000. Accordingly delegates were sent by the company to Holland, and to Hamburg, where rich and adventurous merchants were likely to be found, and where the Scots had considerable trade connections. But in Amsterdam the opposition of the Dutch East India Company prevented any merchants from joining. In Hamburg the money was promised, but in April 1697, Sir Paul Rycaut, the English Resident there, presented an address to the Senate, declaring that the Scots agents had no authority from the King, and that His Majesty would consider any engagement made by the Hamburg merchants with the Scots " an affront " to his authority. The merchants opened a subscription list, but stipulated that no money should be paid until the company should procure a declaration from the King authorising their proceedings. The company, and Parliament on their behalf, presented petitions and addresses to William, begging him to order that all opposition be withdrawn. Although he promised to consider the matter, and to order that his name should not be used to hinder the projects of the company, the Hamburg agent did not withdraw his opposition. No capital was subscribed there, and the Scots were therefore forced to begin operations with their own £400,000, of which only £219,094. 8s. 7d. was actually paid up.

Wherever possible, English opposition thwarted the company. Considering the attitude of England towards Scottish trade since 1660, it was to be expected that a potential rival to the great English companies, with Scottish authority, and with its headquarters in Scotland, would not be allowed to be financed with English capital. Interference abroad, however, was unwarrantable, and deprived Scotland of the last hopes of making the project a success.   In the later conduct of the company's affairs, England could not interfere, until the settlement was made which endangered her foreign relations.   Then William's alarm was justifiable, but not so the measures which were taken against the company and its colony. Although ruin was then inevitable, the conduct of the colonial authorities, acting upon instructions from England, did something to increase the horrors of the desertion of Darien, and much to influence public opinion in Scotland against England, her government, and her people.

When the English voice in the management of affairs was removed, Paterson was able to push his own scheme for a settlement on the Isthmus of Panama, to be a depôt for East and West Indian goods, and to "carry on a Commerce in two vast Continents." The advantages of the scheme to Scotland were said to be many.   A settlement would be provided for her surplus population, to which they should emigrate instead of going to fight on the Continent, or to settle in the English Plantations.   Then the trade which would be attracted to such a settlement would provide a market for Scottish goods, greatly enrich the country, and make her a depôt from which Europe should be supplied with both East and West Indian commodities.   Both silver and gold mines were supposed to exist on the Isthmus; wealth from these was to pour into the country, and Scotland, at one bound, by virtue of this scheme, was to take her position as one of the leading commercial powers of Europe.   Unfortunately there were many weak points in the project.   For one thing, the

amount of capital was utterly inadequate for carrying out
a grandiose plan of this nature. Then, too, the Scots
were inexperienced in the work of colonisation; and also,
but for their trade with the American colonies, they knew
nothing of trade with any countries but those which were
near at hand. Also the spot where they designed to settle
was very near the Spanish settlements of Carthagena,
Panama, and Porto Rico. Paterson, at any rate, ought to
have realised that the exclusive Spanish policy was not
in the least likely to tolerate an alien colony in the midst
of their sphere of influence. The country itself was far
from being the El Dorado of their hopes. The climate
was bad, and the land unfit for a settlement, and the gold
and silver mines were non-existent.

Amongst golden dreams of Scotland's future wealth,
three ships set sail from Leith on 26 July 1698. Early
in November they arrived at the Bay of Acla, in the Gulf
of Darien, where they intended to begin their settlement.
Experience on the voyage had already shewn, what a
short time on shore soon confirmed, the inadequacy of the
regulations made for governing the colony. The supply
of provisions was insufficient; because of carelessness and
dearth no more were sent out from Scotland; and the
goods which had been brought out, including large supplies
of blue bonnets, bibles, and periwigs, were not particularly
suitable for trading with the natives. Pestilence attacked
the small force, and in June 1699, these combined difficulties caused the colonists, now reduced in number from
1200 to 900, to abandon the settlement. The refugees
made for New York, but before they reached that colony,
proclamation had been made, by William's orders, that
his subjects there were to "forbear holding any corre-

spondence with or giving any assistance to " any persons
who had been engaged in making a settlement from
Scotland.   They were able, however, doubtless helped by
their fellow-countrymen settled in New York, to get
enough provisions to take them back to Scotland.

Meanwhile the directors at home had sent out a
second expedition, leaving Leith in May 1699.   They
arrived at New Caledonia, as the settlement had been
named, in August, to find the colony deserted, and after a
short stay they sailed for Jamaica.   The third expedition,
of about 1300 men, sailed from the Clyde in September
of the same year.   Although they had heard rumours of
the desertion of the settlement, they were not prepared
to find that the only remains of the colony, from which
they had hoped so much, were a few empty huts and a
dismantled fort.

The first expedition had already come into collision
with the Spaniards at Carthagena.   A small vessel
belonging to the company was wrecked in the bay, and
the commander and crew were seized as pirates and put
into irons.   They were condemned to be executed, but
owing to English representation the sentence was not
carried out, though they were kept prisoners for a long
time.   Two or three months after the arrival of the third
contingent, the Spanish attack on the intruders, which
had been preparing for a long time, at last took place,
and on 31 March 1700, the settlers finally capitulated[1].

The disastrous end of the first expedition had not
damped the hopes of the Scots, who still looked for
success to crown their endeavours.   The Scots in New

[1] For an account of the different expeditions and the settlements at
Darien, see *Scotland and the Union*, W. Law Mathieson, pp. 33—56.

Jersey were said to be "growne to a very great hight...
from the Success that their Countreymen meet withall in
their settlement of Golden Island[1]." In Scotland there
was said to be "such an earnestness and disposition towards
that matter, without any sparing, either of their persons or
purses, that every observer must think it wonderful[2]."
The news of the final desertion therefore came as an unexpected and very bitter blow to the Scots. Nor had the
English expected their neighbours' enterprise to fail.
The English Parliament had directed their attention to
the Scots Company in its initiatory stages. Then they
had feared that it might be a rival to the East India
Company. Four years later they were again alarmed.
This time they wished to inquire "how consistent the
Colony at Darien may be with the Treaties with Spain
and the Trade of this Kingdom," with special reference
to the Plantation trade[3]. An address on the subject was
sent to the King. In this the Lords expressed their fears
that the settlement might tend "to a disturbance of that
Peace and good Correspondency with the Crown of Spain,
which we conceive is very advantageous to us all"; and
also that it must "prove very inconvenient to the Trade
and Quiet of this Kingdom[4]." William, in his answer,
pointed out the only solution of the difficulty: "His
Majesty does apprehend that Difficulties may too often
arise, with respect to the different Interests of Trade
between His Two Kingdoms, unless some way be found
to unite them more nearly and compleatly[5]." This pro-

[1] *New Jersey Colonial Documents*, ii., p. 288 (June 1699).

[2] *Carstares Papers*, p. 512. Earl of Marchmont to Carstares
(Nov. 1699).

[3] *Lords Journals*, xvi., p. 494.   [4] *Ibid.*, p. 511.

[5] *Ibid.*, p. 514.

posal of union bore no fruit, but it certainly would
not have been a favourable opportunity for approaching
the Scots.

The whole nation was seething with indignation at
the ruin of their cherished scheme, which they attributed
to the malign influence of England. Parliament met in
May 1700, and was overwhelmed with addresses, petitions,
and remonstrances from all parts of the country, begging
that the company's right to the colony of Caledonia
might be maintained, and asserting England's respon-
sibility for its downfall, and the necessity for asserting
Scotland's freedom and independence. Parliament was
adjourned several times, but national excitement did not
abate. In January 1701, Parliament drew up an address
to the King concerning Caledonia. They emphasised the
"several great and grievous hardships" put upon them
by the kingdom of England. These were, firstly, the
interference of both Houses of Parliament in 1695, by
which the company lost subscriptions to the value of
£300,000; and also the address of the Lords to the King,
of February 1700, "persisting in the opposition made
against our Company and their Colony." Secondly,
Parliament complained of the English agent's interference
at Hamburg. Thirdly, the Proclamations issued in the
English colonies were "injurious and prejudicial to the
rights and liberties of the Company[1]." Later, an Act
was passed confirming the privileges and immunities of
the African Company[2].

William never directly answered the address, but in
his last message to the English Parliament a year later,

[1] *Acts, Scotland*, x., p. 248.   [2] *Ibid.*, p. 282.

"His Majesty is fully satisfied that nothing can more contribute to the present and future peace, security and happiness of England and Scotland, than a firm and entire union between them[1]," he again emphasised what he felt would be the only solution of the difficulties of the two countries. In 1702 Anne answered Parliament's address in words of the same tenour: "to avoid all occasions of misunderstanding or differences...we shall think it our happiness to establish an intire Union betwixt the two Kingdomes[2]." With the unsuccessful negotiations for Union of 1702, the history of the African Company is merged into that of the Union. From one point of view, the Darien episode was disastrous indeed; but it was also of use, in that the failure precipitated the crisis in the relations of the two countries. The conception of the scheme, its parliamentary authorisation, the actual settlement in Spanish territory, shewed England that her neighbour might, with favourable conditions, prove a formidable rival. On the other hand, its failure, through want of capital and experience, made plain to the Scots the necessity for money, if their trading interest were to flourish. They had already seen English capital invested in Scottish undertakings; but the experience of the African Company shewed them that the English Parliament would not allow such investments in any scheme which clashed with English interests, and over which it had no control.

[1] *Lords Journals*, xvii., p. 50.   [2] *Acts, Scotland*, xi., p. 14.

CHAPTER VI

THE UNION

THE events of the forty years of commercial and legislative separation, between the Restoration and the accession of Anne, made it very clear that such a relationship could not continue. The interests of the two nations were not identical. England was at war with France, and regarded her as a dangerous commercial rival. England was also attempting to carry out a consistent economic policy, the protection of English commerce and the enlargement of her markets. Of this policy the Navigation Acts embodied an important aspect. On the other hand, one of the principal branches of Scottish commerce was her trade with France, and although it was checked by a war in which she had no interest, it continued to a certain extent in spite of English remonstrances. Scotland was thus the back door through which French influence and prohibited French commodities entered England, and through which, also, English wool was smuggled out of the country to supply the demands of French manufacturers. Then, too, Scotland required markets for the disposal of her manufactures, and therefore she traded with the Plantations, in spite of the

Navigation Acts. Also she had a considerable trade with
Holland, and England feared that, through her, the Dutch
might share in the Plantation trade. The two countries
were governed by different Parliaments, and were under
different trade regulations. The Scottish Parliament
might authorise trade with France, and the export ot
English wool; or might give to a Scots trading company
more extensive privileges than any of the great English
companies possessed. The results of such a grant to a
Scottish company made the necessity for some change in
the relationship of the two countries imminent early in
the eighteenth century, although for some time thought-
ful men on both sides of the border had realised that the
existing state of affairs could not continue. At the same
time the deaths of the little Duke of Gloucester and of
William made the settlement of the succession in the two
kingdoms necessary. In England a complete union was
thought to be the only satisfactory solution of the difficulty. In Scotland opinion differed as to the form of
relationship which should be established. Some desired
an incorporating union, others talked of settling the succession with more limitations on the royal authority, but
all alike desired commercial privileges from England.
Some few contemplated an entire separation, and it was
generally realised that this would mean a revival of the
old connection and alliance with France.

From the time of the Darien disaster until the Union
was actually accomplished, a stream of pamphlets dealing
with the relations of Scotland and England issued from
the Press. All alike declared that the Union had been
unsatisfactory. "That there is a Necessity for Scotland,
either to unite with England or separate from it, is evident

by the Experience of 97 years. In which time this loose and Irregular Tye of the Crowns, in place of an Union of Hearts, Hands and Civil Interest, hath only given Occasion to ill disposed Persons in both Kingdoms to foment continual Jealousies and Animosities betwixt them: And to the English opportunity of crushing every thing that can make for the Interest of Scotland[1]." "For ever since our King's Accession to the Crown of England the English have Always used the Scots, as the Ape did the Cat's clutch, to pull the Chestnuts out of the Fire." Almost all the writers complain of the "preclusions, Restrictions and Hardships which have been put upon them in Matter of Trade since the Restauration[2]." "It is very hard, and ill neighbourhood, neither to allow us a share in their Trade nor to set up for ourselves[3]." Through their union with England the Scots were said to have lost their privileges in France. "Why do we loss the Friendship of all our ancient Allyes for the quarrels betwixt them and England, whilst England gives neither Friendship, free Trade nor priviledges to us[4]." It was said that "without an Inlargement of export it is simply impossible to save us from sinking into the greatest Poverty and Misery." Therefore freedom of trade with the Plantations was especially desired. "This Trade...has all the Advantages that can make a Trade valuable. As First, a Vent for our Home Commodities...Linnen Cloth which...is now become such a drug on our hands, that not a third part is sold of what

---

[1] *An Essay upon the Present State of Scotland* (1700).

[2] *Some Seasonable and Modest Thoughts...concerning the Scots East India Company* (1696).

[3] *The Occasion of Scotland's Decay in Trade* (1705).

[4] *Parainesis Pacifica* (1702).

was formerly...our Stockings, Serges, and Fingrains[1]."
The advantages of union were not to be all on the Scottish
side. England would be "secure within itself, which can
never happen so long as the Interests of England and
Scotland are different[2]." The "Spacious bordering back-
Door" would be "shut against the Evils that otherwise
most fall out." French interference was recognised as being
the principal of these "evils." The Dutch also would be
weakened, for they could be excluded from the Scottish
fisheries, which, for want of capital, the Scots could not
properly work themselves. The result of a union, in fact,
would be "the strengthening of this whole Island in Force
and Riches."

There was a strong Jacobite party opposed to any
scheme of union. Then, too, Scottish antipathy towards
England had been quickened by Glencoe and Darien into
active resentment. Nor were the English sufficiently
aroused to the possibility of danger from their neighbour.
Therefore the Union projects could not be expected to be
drawn up, adopted and welcomed, without much opposition and delay. The first four years of Anne's reign
were occupied in fruitless negotiations and hostile Acts
on the part of both Parliaments, culminating at last in a
determination on both sides to end this state of affairs,
and the preparation and final adoption of a treaty of
Union.

In 1702 the Parliaments of both countries passed Acts
empowering the Queen to appoint Commissioners to treat
for a union[3]. They met in November 1702, and their
discussions turned on the subject of trade. The Scots

---

[1] *Scotland's Interest* (1704).   [2] *The Interest of Scotland* (1700).
[3] *Acts, Scotland,* xi., p. 26; 1 A., c. 8.

demanded free trade between the two countries, equality
of trade with the Plantations, the repeal of the Navigation
Acts, the same import and export regulations and customs
duties for both countries, that neither should be burdened
by the debts of the other contracted before the union,
and that the companies of each kingdom should be unaffected by the union. The English agreed to grant
freedom of trade in all but wool, sheep, and sheep skins.
They hesitated over the Plantation trade, but finally
conceded it. Eventually an agreement was come to on all
points but the last, the continuation of the Scots African
Company. On this subject the Commissioners still differed when the meetings were adjourned in February
1703[1]. They were never resumed, and in September the
Scots Parliament declared the commission for the treaty
to be "terminate and extinct."

In May of the next year a new Parliament met, the
last, and the most important and active of the Scottish
Parliaments. There was a general determination, both
among the people and in Parliament, to make some
change in the relationship of Scotland and England. The
time was favourable for Scotland, for the state of affairs
in England made possible an attempt to wring concessions
from the English Parliament. The death of the Duke of
Gloucester, Anne's child, in 1701, had made some settlement of the succession necessary. Accordingly, by the
Act of Settlement of 1701, the crown was settled upon
the Electress Sophia of Hanover and her heirs, after
Anne's death without direct heirs. It was necessary for
England's welfare that the crown of Scotland should

---

[1] *Acts, Scotland*, xi., App., pp. 149—161.

devolve upon the same person as that of England. But
as yet the Scottish Parliament had taken no steps to
settle the succession. Here, then, was an opportunity for
the Scots. The commercial interests of the two countries
had, by the Darien episode, already been shewn to be conflicting, and many Englishmen were on this account
inclined to union. The Scots had already regretted
that at the Revolution they had not secured commercial
equality from England, in return for their adoption of
William and Mary. Now that the succession question
was again brought forward, they did not intend to allow
the opportunity to slip, " We make but a pitiful Bargain,
if we throw away the present Occasions and Complement
England with entering immediately into the Successions
without the least Equivalent for them. We need not be
at a loss to find out an Equivalent : A freedom of Trade
in general is what we have all along aimed at[1]." The
legislation of the Scottish Parliament in 1703 was, accordingly, inspired by the idea of shewing England that
Scotland could be independent in her choice of a sovereign, and in her arrangements of foreign relations, and
thus of convincing her of the necessity of making commercial concessions.

At the end of William's reign steps had already been
taken in this direction. The Act of 1663, "asserting the
King's prerogative in the ordering of Trade," had been
rescinded, as " prejudicial to the trade of this Nation[2]."
The Lord Chancellor Seafield, in his speech at the opening of the Parliament of 1702, pointed out the necessity
of taking some action to promote trade: " Our manu-

---

[1] *Scotland's Interest* (1704).   [2] *Acts, Scotland,* x., p. 275.

factures," he said, " are very much improved and ought to
have all encouragement but we have almost no Forraign
Trade[1]." Two of the Acts of 1703 and 1704 were aimed
directly at the increase of trade, one allowing the import
of foreign wines, while a second permitted the export of
wool[2]. The " Wine Act " was equivalent to a declaration
of freedom of trade with France, with whom England was
at war. It was supported by the merchants, who suffered
from the Act of 1701 forbidding the import of French
wines; by the government, because the customs on wine
were an important part of the revenue; and by the
Jacobite party, as it gave more opportunities for communi-
cations with the King over the water. The export of wool
was allowed, against the wishes of the manufacturers, to
please the growers and the merchants. Scotland exported
a good deal of her own wool, and also a quantity of English
wool, to Holland and France. This Act therefore affected
also the English manufacturers, a fact which was no doubt
realised by its promoters. One of the pamphleteers of
the time wrote: " Scotland by Allowing this Export may
have a considerable Trade in English Wool....If we neglect
this Opportunity we oblige the English more than we are
sensible: If we make use of it, besides the Money it will
bring into the Country, it may be one of the reasons will
oblige them to drive an Equal Union[3]."

These two Acts shewed the power of Parliament to
regulate trade; the Act of Peace and War asserted its
determination to control foreign relations[4]. This Act

---

[1] *Acts, Scotland*, xi., App., p. 9.   [2] *Ibid.*, pp. 112, 190.

[3] *Letter to a member of Parliament concerning Manufactures and
Trade* (1704).

[4] *Acts, Scotland*, xi., p. 107.

declared that, after Anne's death, "no person being King
or Queen of Scotland and England shall have the sole
power of makeing War" without consent of the Scottish
Parliament, and no declaration of war without their consent was to be binding upon Scottish subjects. The
consent of Parliament was also to be given to all treaties
of peace, alliance or commerce. English statesmen realised
at once the possibility of danger from this Act. Godolphin
wrote to Seafield saying: "The Act for putting the power
of peace and war into the Parliament...might prove ex-
treamly inconvenient both to England and Scotland....
England is now in war with France; if Scotland were in
peace and consequently at liberty to trade with France
would not that immediately necessitate a war betwixt
England and Scotland[1]." But the Act which raised most
commotion, and excited most opposition in the English
Parliament, was the Act of Security, which dealt with the
succession[2]. This declared that, on the death of Anne,
the Scottish Parliament should nominate a successor, who
should not be the same as the successor to the English
crown, unless "during her Majesties reign, there be such
conditions of Government settled as may secure the
honour and sovereignty of this Crown and Kingdom, the
freedom...of Parliament, the religion, liberty and trade of
the Nation from England or any forreigne influence."
A proposed clause, that one of the conditions should
be "that free Communication of Trade the freedome of
Navigation, and the liberty of the Plantations be fully
agreed to," was omitted in the final form of the Act. The
Act of Security was passed in August 1704, and the
English Parliament met at the end of October.

[1] *Stair Annals*, I., App., p. 381.   [2] *Acts, Scotland*, XI., p. 136.

There was much uneasiness about affairs in Scotland. On 23 November Scottish affairs were taken into consideration by the Lords. Lord Haversham made a long speech, in the course of which he said that "there are two matters of all troubles: much discontent, and great poverty; and whoever will now look into Scotland will find them both in that Kingdom." He also declared that in Scotland " there will never be wanting all the promises and all the assistance France will give[1]." The House went into Committee on the question, and addressed Her Majesty to the effect that because of divers Acts recently passed in Scotland, and the " many pernicious and dangerous Effects which are likely to follow from thence, as well in respect to the Trade as to the present and future Peace and Quiet of this Kingdom," they considered themselves " indispensably obliged " to consider means for arresting " such great Evils[2]." The House of Commons also discussed the matter. The result of the deliberations of the two Houses was " An Act for the effectual securing the Kingdom of England from the apparent Dangers that may arise from several Acts lately passed in the Parliament of Scotland[3]." This Act provided first of all that Commissioners should be appointed by the Crown to treat for a " nearer and more compleat Union " with a body of Scottish Commissioners. It went on to declare that, if the succession was not settled in Scotland on the same person as in England, after 25 December 1705, all Scots, except those settled in England or the Plantations or those serving in the army or navy, should be considered aliens. Also, after the same date, no cattle, sheep, or linen

[1] *Parliamentary History*, vi., p. 370.
[2] *Lords Journals*, xvii., p. 607.   [3] 3 & 4 A., c. 6.

should be brought into England from Scotland. Another
Act permitted the export of Irish linen to the Plantations,
at the same time prohibiting the import of Scots linen
into Ireland[1]. Suggestions were also made in the Lords
that ships should be set on the coasts, to take Scots ships
going to or coming from France. The English Parliament
were determined that the Scots should settle the succession
on the Hanover line, and that they should be completely
united with England. "If we do not go into the Succession or an Union very soon, Conquest will certainly be
upon the first Peace[2]," wrote Roxburgh at this time.

The clause of the Act dealing with the import of Scots
linen and cattle into England alarmed the Scots. These
were their most important exports, and "unless our cattle
and linen can be otherwayes disposed on, we are utterly
ruined[3]." Nor could these commodities be sent elsewhere,
for the Scots were already producing more than they could
find a market for. They had endeavoured to coerce the
English into giving them commercial privileges. Now
the English were putting pressure on the Scots to make
them accept a complete union.

An incident occurred about this time which further
convinced statesmen of both countries of the necessity for
union. A vessel belonging to the Scots African Company,
bound for the East Indies, was seized in the Thames, at
the instance of the English East India Company, and detained. A short time later, a vessel called the *Worcester*
put into the Forth for repairs. The Scots believed that

[1] 3 & 4 A., c. 7.

[2] Roxburgh to Baillie. *Correspondence of George Baillie of Jerviswood*
(Bannatyne Club), p. 28.

[3] *Jerviswood Correspondence*, p. 18.

this ship belonged to the English East India Company, and some members of the African Company seized her in reprisal for the seizure of their ship, the *Annandale*. Some idle words of the crew gave rise to the suspicion that the *Worcester* had been a pirate, and had taken a ship, the *Speedy Return*, which the African Company had sent to the East Indies, and had murdered the crew. The captain and the crew of the *Worcester* were tried for piracy, amidst great popular excitement, and condemned to death. The Queen desired that the prisoners should be reprieved, but the Council gave way to the intimidations of the mob, and the captain and two others were hanged. The English were furious at such a sentence being executed on such scanty evidence. The Scots considered that the effort to reprieve the prisoners was a slight upon their African Company, and the relationship between the two countries was still further embittered[1].

About the same time an English man-of-war, anchored in Leith harbour, created great indignation by stopping and searching ships, both Scots and foreign, and also by forcing them to strike to her. A boat's crew was sent aboard a ship from Orkney. To the declaration of the skipper that the cargo consisted of beef, butter, oil and feathers, the Englishman retorted "that he would believe none of our Countrey And y[t] wee had sold our King for a groat, and were arrant knaves and villains." Thereupon a great part of the cargo, including the feathers, was dragged out of the hold and deposited on the deck, with the result that most of it was lost[2]. Incidents such as

[1] For an account of this incident see J. Hill Burton, *History of Scotland*, VIII., pp. 105—108.

[2] *S. P. C. R.*, 12 March 1705.

this did not dispose the Scots to better feeling towards England.

The Scottish Parliament met at the end of June 1705. The Queen's message urged the Estates to consider the questions of succession and union, but they decided that matters relating to trade should first be discussed. Accordingly, proposals made by John Law for establishing a paper credit, and by Hugh Chamberlain for setting up a land bank, were considered. Also an Act was passed appointing a Council of Trade, with very extensive powers. Another Act, which, like the Act of Peace and War, asserted Scottish right to share in the regulation of foreign affairs, provided that a Scots Ambassador must be present at every treaty made with a foreign power. This did not receive the royal assent. Not until the end of August was the question of union taken into consideration, but the business once begun was speedily completed. On 1 September, in spite of strong opposition, the " Act for a treaty with England " was carried[1]. The government were successful in securing that the Commissioners should be appointed by the Queen. A resolution was passed that the Commissioners should not be allowed to meet until the clauses hostile to Scotland in the English Act were repealed. It was moved that this should be included in the Act for a treaty, but fortunately, after much discussion, it was carried that the resolution should form a separate address to the Queen. The objectionable clauses were repealed by the English Parliament in November.

The Commissioners did not meet until April of the next year. After some preliminaries, the English Commissioners proposed that the two kingdoms should be

[1] *Acts, Scotland*, xi., p. 295.

united into one as Great Britain; that they should have
one Parliament; and that the succession in Scotland should
be settled according to the English Act of Settlement.
These were the fundamentals of an incorporating union.
The Scottish proposals, made after a few days' delay, were
that the succession should be settled according to the
English Act, and that there should be free trade between
the two kingdoms and between Scotland and the Plantations. The acquisition of trade privileges was in their
eyes the most important consequence of the Union, while
the English were chiefly anxious to secure, by the union
of the Parliaments, the control over Scottish political
and commercial relations. The Scots soon accepted the
English proposals, insisting on their part on the grant of
free trade, to which the English agreed.

Having decided upon the nature of the Union, it was
necessary to settle the details of the treaty. The questions
of taxation, and of the adjustment of export and import
regulations required much discussion, but both parties
were animated by a sincere desire to come to an agreement, and wise concessions on both sides greatly helped
the negotiations. In the adjustment of the land tax, the
Scots drove a favourable bargain for themselves. In England the total amount was £2,000,000, raised on the basis
of 4s. in the pound. It was arranged that the Scots should
pay £12,000 for each shilling per pound levied in England,
the total therefore being £48,000. With regard to other
taxation, it was decided that the customs and excise should
be the same for both countries. This was of course
necessary for a complete commercial union, but some difficulties arose because Scottish commerce was thus made
liable for paying off the English National Debt, amounting

to over £17,000,000. The total revenue of England was
£5,691,803. 3s. 4½d.; and it was calculated that the Scottish revenue, increasing the land tax from £36,000 to
£48,000, would amount to about £160,000. The lia-
bilities of the country were estimated at about £160,000.
Scottish customs and excise were farmed at £30,000 and
£33,500 respectively; and the same branches of the
revenue in England amounted to £1,341,559 and £947,602.
Elaborate calculations were made as to the extent to which
these two chief branches of the revenue would be burdened
with the payment of the English debt. It was decided
that Scotland, besides being exempted from some taxes
which were shortly to expire, should receive an equivalent in compensation. This was fixed at £398,085. 10s.,
according to the proportion of the Scottish customs
and excise to the several branches of the same revenues
in England which were appropriated to the payment of
the debt. Scotland's own debt of £160,000 was to be
paid from this fund.

One of the taxes from which Scotland was to be
exempted was that on home-made salt. There was
much discussion on this point. The principal ground of
exemption was the poverty of the Scots peasantry, and
the great use they made of salted flesh and fish. As salt
paid a duty in England, arrangements were made for preventing the export of Scots salt to England by land, and
for charging a duty on that exported by sea. As foreign
salt was used in the manufacture of all salted flesh and
fish exported from Scotland, no further duty was charged
on the exportation of these commodities, either to England, the Plantations or other foreign countries. The
Scots Commissioners proposed that the exemption of

Scottish salt from a duty should be perpetual, but the English insisted on limiting its duration to seven years. This article of the treaty was one to which great opposition was afterwards made in Scotland.

When the questions of taxation were settled, the Commissioners had still a few points relating to trade to consider. The existence of the African Company was one of these. It was, of course, impossible that the English Commissioners should allow the company to continue to hold the rights and privileges which had caused so much opposition in England. It was therefore arranged that the shareholders should be bought out, receiving their original capital, and five per cent. interest upon it up to date. This was to be paid out of the Equivalent.

As the Scots were now to come into the English commercial system, it was necessary that their shipping should be regulated in accordance with the English Navigation Acts. The Scots, therefore, proposed that all ships belonging to Scottish subjects, either foreign or native built, should be accounted ships of Great Britain, if they were registered as such within twelve months after the Union treaty was concluded. A large proportion of the ships of Scotland were built abroad, in Holland, Hamburg or the Baltic, and a number of these were part owned by Dutchmen. Therefore the English Commissioners were determined that only ships wholly owned by Scots should be admitted to the register, as they feared that the Dutch might thus thrust themselves into English trade, especially into that to the Plantations. They also insisted that twelve months' grace should not be allowed to the Scottish shipowners, as they might hastily buy more foreign ships, instead of purchasing them from English builders. They therefore fixed the time limit for registration to be the date of the signing of the treaty, afterwards changed by the Scots Parliament to the date of ratification.

These were the most important of the points of the treaty dealing with commerce, and on the whole they were settled impartially and fairly. Nevertheless, a storm of indignation and opposition burst forth in Scotland, partly directed against the idea of union at all, partly against the scheme of an incorporating instead of a federal union; and in those who approved of the Union and the form of it, against the arrangements of the treaty. The commercial clauses in particular were misrepresented and exaggerated, both by public report and by the numerous pamphlets which were issued from the Press. The merchants were assured that no openings would be given them in the great English Companies, that trade to the Plantations was really of no value at all, and that all profitable trade was fully taken up by the English. They were told that they were giving up their freedom of trade with France for a mere shadow, their export trade in wool for a fancied favour, and that the last state of their trade would be infinitely worse than the first. A great deal of the agitation was engineered by the Jacobites; and to their influence, and to the general misrepresentation, must be attributed the address against the Union from the Convention of Royal Burghs, the representative assembly of the trading community. As a matter of fact, however, only twenty-four of the sixty-six joined in the address, and, with the exception of Edinburgh, these were generally poor and unimportant. Edinburgh opposed the Union chiefly because of the loss of her trade, through the removal of Parliament from the city.

As the different clauses became more fully known, were discussed in Parliament and a few alterations made, public opinion veered round, and gradually came to view the treaty with more favour. At bottom, the feeling of the country was really in favour of the Union. As Roxburgh wrote to Baillie in November, 1705: "That an Union will do in the Scottish Parliament I think very probable....The motions will be, Trade with most, Hanover with some, ease and security with others, together with a generall aversion at civill discords, intollerable poverty, and the constant oppression of a bad Ministry[1]."

The changes made in the treaty were not of great importance. A suggestion was made that the export of wool should be allowed, as it was a source of profit to merchants and growers; and the cloth manufacturers, with the competition of English cloth, would not be able to use all the home supply. Such an exception could of course never have been permitted by the English Parliament, and fortunately good sense prevailed, and the attempt to insert this provision into the treaty was given up. An agitation was made for a drawback to be allowed on oats exported from Scotland. The supporters of the motion argued that there was a bounty on the export of corn from England, that Scotland did not export corn, but a considerable quantity of oats, especially to Norway. They also wanted a duty to be imposed on the import of oats from Ireland, which had hitherto been prohibited. This was not incorporated in the treaty, but a bounty was promised on oatmeal exported, of 2s. 6d. per quarter when oats were at 15s. per quarter or under.

---

[1] *Jerviswood Correspondence*, p. 137.

The question of the salt duty was another which was discussed at great length, and which aroused much ill-feeling. In the north, especially in Aberdeenshire, a flourishing trade had recently sprung up in the exportation of salted pork to Holland and to Italy. It was therefore urged that this trade should be encouraged by a drawback, and accordingly the eighth article of the treaty was altered, by a clause which gave 5s. on every barrel of beef or pork salted with foreign salt which was exported, and also of 10s. 5d. on every barrel of white fish. It was also added that Scottish salt, after the expiration of the seven years' exemption, should only be liable to the duty of 12d. per bushel, and not to that of 2s. 4d. The tax on ale had been fixed by the Commissioners at the same rate as that on English strong beer. This was extremely unpopular, and attempts were made to reduce it to the same amount as the tax on English small beer. Pathetic pictures were drawn of the peasant and artisan being deprived of their mug of "tippeny," which naturally appealed to the heart of the lower classes. A compromise was finally effected, chiefly on Defoe's suggestion, and the Scottish tax was fixed midway between those on English strong and small beer. The Act was finally passed by the Scottish Parliament on 16 January 1707. The English Parliament made no changes in the treaty, and on 6 March the Queen gave the royal assent to the Act of Union in the Parliament of England; and the long chapter of partial union, with separate interests and authorities and many misunderstandings, was at last at an end.

But the conclusion of the treaty was far from being the immediate beginning of a golden period of prosperity and agreement. There was yet much mutual dislike and

distrust, and there were to be many difficulties and con-
flictions of interest. The consummation of a complete
union was in itself the immediate cause of a dilemma in
commercial affairs. Already, in 1705, queries had been
put to the English Privy Council as to the question of
the import of certain goods to England from Scotland;
commodities which were prohibited altogether in England;
or which only paid a small duty in Scotland, and were
liable to a heavy duty in England; or Plantation goods
which were supposed to be brought straight to England
from America[1]. The decisions of the Council do not
seem to have been made public, at any rate they were
disregarded. They had declared that French goods might
not be brought into England from Scotland under any
circumstances. The Scots merchants, however, considered
that it would be a paying transaction to bring large
quantities of French goods into Scotland, paying a low
duty, and, as soon as the Union treaty was concluded, to
carry them over the border and get a good price in England. They therefore proceeded to import large quantities
of wines. Defoe wrote in February 1707 to Godolphin,
from Edinburgh, "Your Lordship knows well that in this
place there is an open trade with France. And as this
trade is very considerable so on the prospect of a Union I
perceive there are several wheels at work to lay schemes
of private trade from hence for England."

English merchants, too, soon saw the possibilities of
gain in this trade, and hastened to share in it. Defoe in
the same letter says, "But the main particular I give you
this trouble upon is this, here are great commissions from
London already for the buying up wines and brandies on the

[1] *Treasury Books, Outletters, Customs*, XIV., 35.

supposition that they shall be freely conveyed to England after the Union and that England will not so far disoblige Scotland at first as to obstruct it…if they are assured of a liberty…your Lordship will find the inconvenience very great and the quantity before the 1st of May incredible[1]." Defoe was anxious that, if this trade was to be allowed, his patron Harley should profit by it. "If it shall pass into England why shall your honour not permit me to buy you a tun of rich claret here, which I may do as cheap as you buy a hogshead, and I'll take my hazard that it shall be extraordinary on my own risk[2]." As 1 May, when the treaty was to come into force, approached, French commodities came in in still greater quantities. On 22 April Defoe wrote: "the foundation laid here for clandestine trade is beyond all this, fatal to both the revenue and to trade…nor do I see any possibility of wholly preventing it, without an army of officers[3]."

Those London merchants who had nothing to do with the trade petitioned the House of Commons to interfere. They passed a bill to prohibit any French goods at all from being brought into England from Scotland, but this was rejected by the Lords, because of the clamour which it raised in Scotland. There they complained that the English did not intend to keep the treaty, and that those commercial privileges which had been held out to them were already being nullified. In June forty ships from Scotland with French wines and brandies arrived in the Thames, where they were seized by the customs officers. The outcry in Scotland was now redoubled. The petition

---

[1] *H. M. C. R., Portland Papers*, IV., p. 388.

[2] *Ibid.*, p. 392. Defoe to Harley (10 March 1707).

[3] *Ibid.*, p. 403. Defoe to Harley.

of the merchants who owned the ships and cargoes expressed the popular feeling. They said they sent certain goods which were allowed to be imported into Scotland before the Union, having paid her Majesty's duties, to London, with the usual coquets in order. "But to our great surprise we have informatione that not only our ships and goods are seized but the goods themselves made havock of and imbaizled (expressly contrair to the articles of union) our seamen impressed and our Ships therby rendered useless, which treatment is so unsupportable that all those promised advantages of the union are like to be so many traps to ensnare us which in the end must turn to our inevitable ruine, for if our effects be seized and our ships laid up and taken from us by violence where shall we have any hopes left us for trade[1]." After a good deal of discussion between the customs authorities the Attorney-General and the Judges, and Parliament, the proceedings were ultimately stayed by order of the House of Commons, the ships released and the cargoes restored; but nevertheless the incident caused much discontent in Scotland[2].

The adjustment of the fiscal relations of the two countries was a matter of considerable difficulty. The Scots custom and excise had been farmed out to individuals, who, as long as they made a comfortable profit for themselves, were not at all particular, either about the enforcement of regulations, or the exact collection of the duties. Therefore, when both branches of the revenue were assimilated with the English revenue and were

---

[1] *Royal Burghs*, iv., p. 416.

[2] For a full account of this affair see Mackinnon, *History of the Union*, pp. 353—361.

managed by a body of English and Scottish Commissioners, who appointed many English officials to introduce
the new methods, and to see that the new duties were
properly collected, there was widespread alarm and disgust
amongst the trading classes. Smuggling had always been
a profitable occupation; it was infinitely more so since the
introduction of the higher English duties. From the
reports of the customs officials in North Britain it is evident that the trade in French wine and brandy had by
no means come to an end. Large quantities were still
imported all round the coast; and wool, under cover of
being taken to other Scottish ports, was sent abroad. The
Commissioners wrote that "the naturall situation of this
Countrey doth very much perplex Us being so many and
such large inletts which are as it were so many Seas, and
scarce ever free of great Gusts and dark Cold nights,
and by reason of the Mighty Ebbs most of the Shoars are
dangerous. As hardship of weather wee doubt too often
hinders the officers from watching the Coast so what terri-
fies them most, the Countrey people all side with the
Smuglers[1]." Smuggling was of course very common in
England also at this time, but just after the Union it
seems to have been even more prevalent in Scotland than
was usual in the eighteenth century. The new and higher
duties, the endeavour to exact them fully, organised
attempts to put down smuggling, and the introduction of
English officials, were all extremely unpopular.

A temporary source of misunderstanding was the delay
in the payment of the Equivalent, and when it did arrive,
although the payment of the African Company's stock
was most welcome, it was a long time before any of the

[1] *Treasury Papers*, cxvi., 4.

money was applied to the encouragement of manufactures. And industry certainly suffered from the immediate effects of the Union. The Scottish cloth manufacturers could not compete with the English cloth, which now came freely into the country, and some of the newly introduced manufactures suffered greatly from English competition. They had been reared under a strongly protective system, and the first blast of free competition caused them to wither for a time. Not even freedom of trade to the Plantations and a greatly enlarged market could at first compensate the manufacturers. Altogether, for several years after the Union the country did not appear to profit much by it, at any rate from an industrial point of view. But trade and shipping began very soon to improve—the amount of trade with the Plantations increasing very quickly. The development of the great trade of Scotland with the West, begun amidst difficulties, and carried on for a time in spite of English opposition, was one of the most important results of the Union. But the Union does not depend for its justification on the results of one or another provision, but on its consequences to the prosperity and welfare of the kingdom as a whole. Scotland obtained opportunities for industrial and commercial development. England gained security from France, and stability for her commercial system, but still more important has been the development and progress of both as the United Kingdom of Great Britain.

BIBLIOGRAPHY

MANUSCRIPTS.

State Papers. Domestic. 1603–1707. (Public Record Office.)
State Papers. Colonial. 1603–1707. (Public Record Office.)
Treasury Papers. 1660–1707. (Public Record Office.)
Customs Accounts. Inspector-General's Ledger of Imports and
    Exports. 1697–1707. (Public Record Office.)
Register of the Scottish Privy Council. 1661–1678; 1682–1685;
    1689–1707. (General Register House.)
Customs and Excise Accounts. 1603–1707. (General Register House.)
Parliamentary Papers. 1603–1707. (General Register House.)
Harleian MSS. 1314; 1324. (British Museum.)
Additional MSS. 28079; 21133. (British Museum.)
Maitland and Lauderdale MSS. 35125, f. 210. (British Museum.)

PRINTED RECORDS.

Acts of the Parliament of Scotland.
Register of the Scottish Privy Council. 1603–1660.
Records of the Convention of the Royal Burghs of Scotland.
Statutes of the Realm.
Scobell's Collection of Acts and Ordinances.
Calendar State Papers. (Spanish.)
Calendar State Papers. (Venetian.)
Thurloe State Papers.
Journals of the House of Commons.
Journals of the House of Lords.

Historical Manuscripts Commission Report :
    House of Lords MSS.
    MSS. of the Duke of Portland.
    MSS. of the Duke of Buccleugh and Queensferry.
    MSS. of the Earl of Mar and Kellie.
    MSS. of the Earl of Carlisle.
Proclamations. (British Museum.)
New York Colonial Manuscripts.
New Jersey Colonial Documents.

HISTORIES, ARTICLES, Etc.

Alexander, W., Earl of Stirling. Register of Royal Letters.
Ashley, W. J. Surveys, Historic and Economic.
Baillie of Jerviswood. Correspondence of. (Bannatyne Club.)
—— Robert. Letters and Journals. (Bannatyne Club.)
Balfour, Sir James. Historical Works. (Annals.)
Bingham, H. The Early History of the Scots Darien Company.
    (Scottish Historical Review, Vol. III.)
Brown, P. Hume. Scotland in the Time of Queen Mary.
—— (ed.). Early Travellers in Scotland.
Burnet. History of his own Times.
Burton, J. Hill. History of Scotland.
Carlyle, T. Cromwell's Letters and Speeches.
Carroll, B. R. Historical Collections of South Carolina.
Carstares Papers.
Chalmers. Political Annals of the Present United Colonies. (1780.)
—— G. History of the Revolt of the American Colonies.
Child, Josiah. New Discourse of Trade.
Clément, P. Histoire du Système Protecteur en France.
Collins, John. Salt and Fishery. (1682.)
Cunningham, W. Growth of English Industry and Commerce.
Darien Papers. (Bannatyne Club.)
Davidson, J. and Gray, A. Scottish Staple at Veere.
Defoe, D. History of the Union of England and Scotland.
Firth, C. H. Scotland and the Commonwealth. (Scottish History
    Society.)
—— Scotland and the Protectorate. (Scottish History Society.)

Fischer, Th. A. Scots in Germany.
—— Scots in East and West Prussia.
—— Scots in Sweden.
Fletcher, A. First and Second Discourses concerning the affairs of Scotland.
Francisque-Michel. Les Écossais en France.
Historical Account of the Staple Contract between the Burrows of Scotland and Campvere.
Hutchinson Papers. (Prince Society.)
Lamont, John. Diary of. (Maitland Club.)
Lauderdale Papers. (Camden Society.)
Letters and State Papers during the reign of James I. (Abbotsford Club.)
Mackenzie, Sir George. Memoirs of the affairs of Scotland from the Restoration.
Mackinnon, J. Union of England and Scotland.
Macleod, H. D. Theory and Practice of Banking.
McUre, J. History of Glasgow.
Massachusetts Historical Society Collections.
Mathieson, W. Law. Scotland and the Union.
Nicoll, John. Diary of public transactions. 1649-1666. (Bannatyne Club.)
Scott, W. R. Scottish Industrial Undertakings before the Union. (Scottish Historical Review, Vols. II. and III.)
—— (ed.). Minutes of New Mills Cloth Manufactory. (Scottish History Society.)
Spottiswoode. History of the Church and State of Scotland.
Stair Annals.
Terry, C. S. The Cromwellian Union. (Scottish History Society.)
Tucker, T. Report upon Settlement of Revenues of Excise and Customs in Scotland. (Bannatyne Club.)
Webster. History of the Presbyterian Church in America.
Wedderburne, David. Compt Buik of. (Scottish History Society.)
Whitehead, W. A. East Jersey under the Proprietary Government.

TRACTS.

Case of Scotsmen residing in England and in the English
    Plantations. (Advocates' Library.)
Essay upon Industry and Trade. (Advocates' Library.)
Essay upon the Present State of Scotland. (1700.)
Grants, Concessions and Original Constitutions of the Province
    of New Jersey.
Interest of Scotland. (1700.)
Letter to a Member of Parliament concerning Manufactures and
    Trade. (1704.) (Advocates' Library.)
Proceedings of the Parliament of Scotland Begun at Edinburgh,
    6th May, 1703. (Advocates' Library.)
Parainesis Pacifica ; or, A Perswasive to the Union of Britain.
    (1702.)
Representation of the Advantages of Manufactories. (1683.)
Scotland's Interest.... (1704.)
Scotland's Grievances Relating to Darien.
Some Seasonable and Modest Thoughts...concerning the Scots
    East India Company. (1696.)
The Occasion of Scotland's Decay in Trade.... (1705.)

Printed in the United States
By Bookmasters